Stop Anger
Be Happy!

Kathy S. Garber
Licensed Marriage and Family Therapist

Contact the author at:
http://www.AngerManagementOnline.com

Kathy Garber
Stop Anger, Be Happy

Ebook and website design: Advanced Design
http://www.d50.com

Order this book online at www.trafford.com/02-0809
or email orders@trafford.com

Most Trafford titles are also available at major online book retailers.

Note for Librarians: A cataloguing record for this book is available from Library
and Archives Canada at www.collectionscanada.ca/amicus/index-e.html

National Library of Canada Cataloguing in Publication
Garber, Kathy
            Stop anger, be happy / Kathy Garber.ISBN
            1. Anger. I. Title.

BF575.A5G37 2002   152.4'7   C2002-904430-8

Printed in Victoria, BC, Canada.

ISBN: 978-1-55395-095-0

*We at Trafford believe that it is the responsibility of us all, as both individuals
and corporations, to make choices that are environmentally and socially sound.
You, in turn, are supporting this responsible conduct each time you purchase a
Trafford book, or make use of our publishing services. To find out how you are
helping, please visit www.trafford.com/responsiblepublishing.html*

*Our mission is to efficiently provide the world's finest, most comprehensive
book publishing service, enabling every author to experience success.
To find out how to publish your book, your way, and have it available
worldwide, visit us online at www.trafford.com/10510*

 www.trafford.com

North America & international
toll-free: 1 888 232 4444 (USA & Canada)
phone: 250 383 6864 ♦ fax: 250 383 6804 ♦ email: info@trafford.com

The United Kingdom & Europe
phone: +44 (0)1865 722 113 ♦ local rate: 0845 230 9601
facsimile: +44 (0)1865 722 868 ♦ email: info.uk@trafford.com

Introduction

Many people have asked me throughout the years how I became involved in teaching anger management and why I enjoy working with angry people. My interest in teaching anger management flourished when I started working with adults who were experiencing huge difficulties or road blocks in their lives as a result of their angry behavior. Some of the clients I worked with in anger issues lost jobs or company promotions. Others spent time in court explaining their angry behavior and suffering humiliation for the circumstances bringing them before the legal system. Many of these same individuals lost important relationships: a spouse, partner, friends, co-workers and even the respect of their children. Oddly enough, most of these same people are some of the nicest and most sincere people I had ever met in my life. I began to wonder; where does it all go wrong for them?

In working with angry individuals I came to understand that angry people aren't really "bad" people, as they may have been labeled, or people who should be suffering from loss or humiliation, but people who need help in learning to express their uncomfortable emotions appropriately. When you really think about it, how many of us have been taught how to deal with our emotions or anger at all? The majority of us have been taught to suppress anger because it isn't socially acceptable to feel angry or it's not "nice" to feel angry. Even worse than being told that you need to suppress anger is being told it is wrong to have anger in the first place. Being told that your emotions are wrong leads to even more guilt and stress. Rather than totally eliminating your anger I want to help you understand that you can have appropriate anger and deal with it in healthy ways.

In working with you in anger management, I want to offer solutions and alternatives to your unsuccessful behaviors. I want to become a co-creator with you to generate real change in your life. I believe that you are capable of powerful change if you have a desire and willingness to participate in those changes.

In order for real behavioral change to take place, the anger management techniques you practice must be "right" for you and your life. The techniques or solutions need to come from self investigations of your life and your own frame of reference. Self investigation requires you to focus on your life and decide what behaviors aren't working for you any longer and how you can make changes in your life to become successful in handling your emotions.

Taking a good hard look at yourself is difficult work and if you aren't willing to do your share of work in this program, you probably won't be very successful in anger management. I don't mean that statement to discourage you in your process of change, but to let you know that the work we do here is really up to you. I can coach you along in the process and provide information, but the changes you desire really come from you implementing the program ideas into your life and finding solutions that feel good in your life.

Creating serious behavioral change requires that you become very proactive in the process. You have to decide what you need and want in your life. Only you hold the answers to your life and this anger management program is a stepping stone to get you excited about the possibilities of achieving anger control designed by you and with an anger management coach.

There are many different thoughts regarding anger management and the way it is presented to clients and students. After doing my own research of various anger management techniques and programs I realized that all people are capable of great change in behavior if they were able to focus on and recognize the behaviors that needed to be changed for themselves. In working with anger sufferers, I recognized the fact that people are more willing to alter their behaviors if they can make changes on their own terms and operate within their own frame of reference. In working with anger suffers, I also realized that people need to feel empowered in their life to make changes in their behavior; not simply told how to make changes that suit someone else's life style. Anger management is about living in solutions that feel "right" in your own life.

The task of learning anger management isn't an easy process, however, with the right tools and a supportive environment you can determine the areas of your life which are calling out for your attention and then learn how to go about making those changes.

In writing *Stop Anger, Be Happy,* I want to validate your anger and let you know that having anger is a normal part of life, but you don't have to stay a victim to your anger and allow it to remain uncontrolled. And, I want to help you become honest in the process by admitting you have a problem with anger and finding solutions to help balance out your emotions.

I also wrote *Stop Anger, Be Happy* for the following reasons:

1. I want to help you understand the emotion of anger doesn't necessarily have to be a horrible experience. It is how you react or act out the anger that counts.

2. I want anger sufferers to know that having anger is a normal part of life, but the actions or behaviors you may be attaching to it may not serve you well as an adult.

3. I want to offer solutions and alternatives which will allow you to have your emotions while remaining in control of your life.

4. I want to help you work through acceptance of your anger problem and work toward healthy solutions.

5. I want to show you how important getting active in your own life can lead to a better understanding of your emotions.

6. I want you to know that your life can change if you are willing to move on from your anger and find better ways to express yourself.

How the Book Is Organized

Stop Anger, Be Happy is geared to be user friendly, and offer a straight forward approach for anger management. It starts off by asking you to monitor your behavior and to keep a journal of your emotions. The book helps you to understand your warning signs and anger triggers. It teaches you how to deal with your anger at lower levels so that you can gain control quickly instead of letting your anger build to the point of explosion. We will be discussing relaxation techniques and their daily benefits. *Stop Anger, Be Happy* will help you to determine the behaviors that are not working for you as an adult and replace them with new and successful ways of handling your anger.

This book also teaches you about successful communication and how to set boundaries so that you get what you need and want in your life. It is a tool to get you thinking about your life, your behavior and it motivates you to make change so that you can stop taking up your time feeling angry and start living your life to its fullest potential. *Stop Anger, Be Happy* and AngerManagementOnline.com encourage self forgiveness and self kindness in your process of change. Both the book and the class empower you to build self esteem and aid you in realizing that your mistakes are here today, but how you live in your future is what really counts.

There is no doubt that examining and changing your own behavior is never an easy process, nor will you learn about your anger and become proficient in successful anger management techniques overnight. However, with hard work, dedication and desire, there is no doubt that you can do it. No matter what you are thinking right now or where you are at in your life, you are capable of making great change and living the life you desire.

For more help with anger management, I have developed a website http://www.AngerManagementOnline.com   AngerManagementOnline.com is a place where individuals working with anger issues can discuss this book and find support from others. The program can be completed in the comfort of your own home when you are ready to learn at a time that is convenient to you. The completely online community offers discussion boards closely moderated by an anger management facilitator, use of a live chat room and email correspondence with an anger facilitator. You can request progress reports and a certificate of completion once you have met the program requirements and your facilitator feels you have successfully learned anger management. People use this program for court requirements, human resource referrals and for self improvement. You will find some of the hardest working individuals in behavioral change in the discussion boards exchanging information, problems and solutions. AngerManagementOnline.com is a supportive environment designed to welcome all who seek help in managing their anger. Working through this book with a therapist or counselor is highly encouraged

The ultimate goal in anger management is not to eliminate your anger; rather, your goal in anger management is to learn how to understand and express your feelings in healthy ways that will allow you to gain the outcomes you desire. Learning to experience your feelings and expressing them in healthy ways is not a simple process; it is a life long process. Let's get started now in that process…

This book is dedicated to
my parents
Grover and Janice Garber in appreciation for all their hard work and dedication in making
my life a happy place to exist.

And to God
from whom all my life's blessings have come.

Stop Anger
Be Happy!

Table of Contents

Chapter 1

Anger Is A Fact of Life

If you are reading this book, there is a good chance that you (or someone you care about) have an anger problem. An anger problem exists when people become dependent on anger as a primary means of expressing themselves; when they inappropriately use anger or the threat of violence as a weapon to get their way. Inappropriate and uncontrolled anger is harmful for both targets of anger and the angry person as well. Inappropriate anger destroys relationships, makes it difficult to hold down a job, and takes a heavy toll on your physical and emotional health.

Everyone has issues and concerns about anger. Some people may need help in managing anger that gets out of control; others need help in accessing buried anger. Some take their anger out on innocent people and others take their anger out on themselves with smoking, drinking alcohol, binge eating, overeating or bombarding themselves with self criticism. Others pretend they aren't angry but then get back at those who hurt or threaten them in indirect and underhanded ways, such as gossiping, being sarcastic, or distancing themselves.

You simply cannot avoid anger in your life and my goal in working with you is not to make you anger free or rid you of your angry feelings. Rather I am going to help you acknowledge your anger; understand your anger and ultimately you will gain control of it.

This first chapter is geared toward getting you ready and excited to learn anger management. You will notice that the book works slowly through the process of anger management. Anger management is just like any other treatment plan you have ever followed in your life. You have to follow the process step by step in order to get the desired results. Believe me, there are no short cuts to understanding your emotions or changing your behavior.

Most people come to me and want a quick fix for their anger issues and fast answers to put an end to their vicious cycle of uncontrolled behavior. I think we want results right now because we live in a fast paced society and we are used to getting everything right now. I also think by the time people start becoming curious about their anger they are starting to lose important things in their lives and they want to "fix it" fast. The real truth is there are no quick answers to the work you are doing here. You are on a journey of self improvement and you will reap the rewards of working slowly and carefully through the book.

Stop Anger, Be Happy is a program that guides you slowly through the process of looking at how anger affects and shapes your life. I will encourage you to look deep inside to explore the roots of your anger and evaluate what your anger says about you as a person.

As I outlined in the Introduction of this book, I am going to work *with* you as a coach helping you to learn new behavioral techniques and setting new goals in your life. As your coach, I will guide you in the journey and work with you as a co-creator in making the changes you desire in your life. Your responsibility in the learning process will be doing the most difficult part of the work by implementing the techniques and solutions you decide work best for you into your daily life. Implementing anger management techniques into your life will mean; practicing, failing, practicing, and experiencing success, practicing, failing and feeling successful again. There will be times when your behavioral changes will leave you feeling successful and on top of the game and then there will be times when you implement a change that will leave you feeling like a failure. It is very important for you to keep in mind that you *are* learning new information about yourself and growing in the process even during the times you *think* you failed.

Behavioral change can leave you feeling as though you are sailing smoothly down the hills of life with the greatest of ease learning and growing and other times you are going to think you are climbing the highest mountain in your life while trying to stay focused and on track in the program. In the very beginning phases of anger management you might compare your process of change to the longest roller coaster ride you have ever been on in your life! The key to success in any process of change is riding the ups and downs and hanging in there for the duration of the ride. You must hang on and stay dedicated in this process to make the changes you desire in your life.

Our Goals

Working with you as an anger management coach does not mean that I am going to find all of the right answers *for* you. Rather, my goal in working with you is to cut right to the chase and get busy in the learning process early on in the program with you as a willing participant looking for answers that fit you and your life. Another goal I strive for in teaching anger management is building a working relationship so that we can work together in honesty for the common goal of your self improvement, behavioral change, and anger control.

As your anger management coach, I want to get down to the task of looking at what needs to be changed, what you want to change and how you are going to achieve those changes in your life from the very beginning of the program. The changes you want to make in your behavior require that you look at yourself with openness and gut level honesty. After all, you are the only one who knows which behaviors need to be changed to make your life a more successful place to live and you are also the only one who can make those changes. No one can do that work for you.

Looking At Yourself

Admitting that your behavior needs to be changed is one of the toughest parts of anger management and the point where most people want to give up and automatically throw in the towel. Looking at yourself and your behavior is not an easy task, but a very necessary one if you want to make the changes you desire. You might not be able to admit to a loved one or friends that you have a problem with anger, but you really need to get honest with yourself to move forward in this program.

My name is _____ and I have a problem controlling my anger.

Let's face it…looking at yourself or making changes in your behavior is not an easy task; however, if you are willing to examine the things that aren't working in your life you will become successful in controlling your anger. To become successful in controlling your anger, you must first make the effort to understand your feelings, admit your emotions and behaviors before you can make powerful changes in your life. The good news is you *are* capable of great change if you are willing to take responsibility in this process.

Anger…

Now that you know how this program is going to work and you have accepted the responsibility of learning anger management, let's shift gears and think about anger.

The number of angry people of all ages and backgrounds expressing anger in the form of violence is increasing everywhere: work, home, shopping centers, schools, and highways to name just a few. Literally millions of people have serious problems managing and keeping anger under their own control and yet very few do anything to change their behavior until they have encountered a significant loss. If you feel as though you are one of those millions suffering as a result of your angry behavior, you are ready to start the process of change.

Although the emotion of anger is an age old problem, the world we now live in is more complex than ever before. Daily situations have become more and more irritating causing more stress and more angry behavior. Take a second and think of a time recently when you experienced an episode of anger. I am fairly confident that you could quickly muster up a thought or two of recent encounters with rude people, traffic jams, incompetent co-workers, road hogs and the least of our favorites, critical people. When these stressful encounters happen over and over again in your daily routine it is easy to understand why millions of people experience and suffer from anger.

You may be thinking that you can't avoid all the situations, people or triggers mentioned above that bring on your angry feelings. While you might not be able to avoid *all* the triggers and stressors in your life, you *are* capable of learning what your triggers are, how to change the patterns of your thinking and the way in which you chose to display your anger. You *are* capable of becoming proactive in your life and finding solutions that will make you successful in anger management.

Anger Is Normal

Did you think you would be learning that anger is a normal emotion in an anger management program? The emotion of anger is a completely normal, usually healthy, human emotion. Anger is a basic emotion that is experienced by all people. Typically triggered by an emotional hurt, anger is usually experienced as an unpleasant feeling that occurs when we think we have been injured, mistreated, opposed, or when we are faced with obstacles that keeps us from attaining personal goals.

The experience of anger varies widely. How often anger occurs, how intensely it is felt and how long it lasts is different for each of us. Anger is also different for each of us in how easily we get angered, as well as how comfortable we are with feeling angry. Some people are always getting angry while others seldom feel angry. Some of you are very aware of your anger, and others of you fail to recognize your anger at all.

Anger can be constructive or destructive. Anger can be a signal to you that something in your environment isn't right. It captures your attention and motivates you to take action to correct what is bothering you.

Some of our greatest changes and movements throughout history have taken place because of anger generating motivation for change. Anger can serve as a great motivator, however, if you do more than simply talk about your anger, or strive for change as a result of your anger you risk causing destruction to yourself and others in your life. Just as anger can serve as a motivator, it can also become your most destructive emotion if left unattended on automatic pilot. As an adult, it is your responsibility to first learn what triggers your anger and then work toward developing strategies to keep those triggers from tipping you over the edge. Your goal is to *understand* your emotions and not simply to act out your bad feelings.

The truth is… we all feel angry at times. Wouldn't you agree? Like any other emotion (happiness, fear, sadness…), we each experience and express anger at different levels. Some people tend to become angry very easily "hotheaded" while some are not quick to show anger, but have problems keeping their anger under their own control. Others tend to take the spotlight off of their behavior and blame people for causing them to act in certain ways rather than taking responsibility for their own actions. It doesn't really matter if you are slow to anger, quick to anger or think you never really show anger at all. You have anger and it's all the same emotion. It just gets displayed differently.

Some people want to believe that they do not have a problem with anger even though others in their life are telling them to get help with their behavior. A loved one or co-worker may have even suggested that you take a look at your behavior or that you should participate in an anger management program. Often this suggestion totally baffles the

4

unsuspecting person on automatic pilot or the person who isn't paying attention to his own life. Some people argue that they don't have anger because they don't show it. They keep it inside so they must not have anger right?

Even the people who don't "show" their anger experience the emotion of anger. You might be thinking to yourself: If these people don't openly show anger, where is their anger? How can I express my anger so openly that it causes me problems and others seem as though they don't experience anger at all. Let me assure you that everyone experiences anger, but the actual display of anger varies among individuals. People who deny that they feel anger hide or bottle up their emotions so tightly inside of them it is like a vibrating volcano ready to spew hot lava all over the next person or event that causes them stress or frustration. Or, maybe they do continue to hide their anger and it continues to fester and in turn cause a multitude of health problems and low self-esteem because their needs are never met. The only difference in hiding your anger deep inside or "letting it all hang out" is that you are the only victim of your anger, but make no mistake about it, you do have anger. We all have and experience the emotion of anger.

No matter how you learned to display your anger in the past, it is time to start fresh and learn healthy new behaviors to replace the old unsuccessful behaviors you have carried around for a very long time. It is time to learn and grow in your life. It is time to shed the old learned behaviors from years ago and replace them with healthy behaviors that you develop during your self examination and self study in this program. It is time to stop blaming or finding fault with how you learned your behavior. It is time for you to be kind to yourself in this process of difficult change and grow toward self understanding and empathy. It is time to forgive yourself and move on.

The Price You Pay

Who doesn't like to shop around for a good deal to save money? Who wants to pay a high price for something we can get cheaper somewhere else? Discount stores even help us out by price matching, strategically offering low cost items and price planning. When it comes to saving money, we make every effort to find a good product at a fair cost. We get all wrapped up in the search for the best deal in town and most of us make it a challenge to keep money in our own pockets.

The question to ask your self is this: why are we so willing to search for good deals and low prices to keep money in our pockets, but so willing to pay a huge cost for our angry/bad behavior? Have you ever shopped around for good deals on ways to change or learn good behavior before you absolutely were forced to do so? Who looks around for that good deal on anger management until it actually costs you something or you are forced into taking the class? Anger management isn't something we normally search out unless we absolutely need it or are forced into it by the legal system, human resources or loved ones as an ultimatum to loss.

The point is this: anger, if it hasn't already, will eventually cost you something. Angry behavior usually carries a very high price tag and once the damage is done there aren't many good deals to find or ways of repairing the damage unscathed. Ask yourself: what is the highest price you are willing to pay to allow your anger to stay unmanaged or uncontrolled? What are you willing to lose before you look for the good deal in anger management? Family? Friends? Loved ones? Partner? Job? Children? Respect? Self esteem?

What expenses might you have already encountered by not managing your anger? Court costs? Repair costs of the destruction performed while you were angry? Legal fees? Hurt feelings of loved ones and friends? Loss of a promotion? Shame? Guilt? The list could go on and on, but the ultimate price you could pay is a relationship with a loved one. There is usually loss involved with uncontrolled anger, but you don't have to suffer loss when you are capable of great change.

Can you identify yourself in any of the facts or situations below?

- Anger has consequences, and usually involves hurting other people emotionally or physically.
- Anger can affect your work costing you earned promotions and leave you with feelings of guilt and shame.
- As a result of your anger, co-workers or loved ones may not want to be around you fearing that your anger will become out of control.
- Friends decline your invitations fearing your unpredictable anger.
- Your kids make excuses not to go places with you.

Take a moment now and think of a price you may have paid for your angry behavior. Ask yourself: What price did you pay to express your anger? What did it cost you? What have you lost as a result of not controlling your anger? Take a moment now and write a paragraph about your anger, its affect on your life and what it has cost you. Below that paragraph, write about the changes you want to make and where you see your life in the future. There is a bright future when you are willing to do the work and make powerful, positive changes in your life.

The price I paid for my anger:

_____
_____
_____
_____

The changes I want to make in my behavior:

_____
_____
_____
_____
_____

Why Are You Reading This Book?

You may be reading this book because it is obvious that the way you are currently handling your anger isn't working for you anymore. Others may be forced into reading this book or taking anger management classes and it is not so obvious to you why you are here or why you even need to do this work. Maybe a loved one or co-worker told you to get help in managing your emotions. Maybe the legal system or a human resources department told you to get your anger under control and you feel forced into making changes.

If it is not obvious to you why you are taking anger management, it will become clearer the deeper into this process you delve. Be open to the possibility that some of your old behaviors may need to be changed in order to gain control of your anger and your other emotions.

Let's be clear and honest. Your behavior isn't going to change overnight. And again, this is where anger management takes a bad rap. Some people put in one or two days of hard work and expect to see fantastic results. Remember, you didn't learn to become the person you are today overnight. It was a process of learning, growing and surviving in the world. Successful anger management or any behavioral change for that matter is a process of small baby steps and staying with the process no matter how rough it feels.

This anger management program is designed so that you work slowly and build a strong and unwavering foundation before moving on in the program. To be successful in behavioral change you will need to stick with the process no matter how hard it becomes. There will be days when your successes are evident and you will be proud of yourself and there will be days when your failures will be right in your face letting you know that you slipped. The important part is that you hang on and keep trying. Remember that roller coaster?

Begin this process by making a commitment to think about your behavior every day. Think about how you are acting or reacting to situations in your life. Take the challenge of pausing to engage your rational brain to think before acting out your emotions. This is a process of desire, awareness, renewal, and change.

Do You See What They See?

Sometimes your anger is more obvious to those around you than it is to yourself. You have been living with your same behaviors all of your life and are probably very used to your actions and re-actions, however, someone you work with or live with is encouraging you to make changes in your behavior. **Think:** Why is someone suggesting I look at my behavior? Is it possible that they could be suffering along with me as a result of my anger? Remember, anger affects everyone in its proximity. If you are displaying anger, others are seeing your anger and feelings its repercussions.

If someone has told you or is telling you over and over again that you display bad behavior when you are angry, maybe its time that you give it some thought. Maybe their suggestion will start you on the path of thinking about your behavior and taking responsibility for it.

One of the hardest things to admit is that other's can see qualities in you that you may not be able to see in yourself. You may perceive someone telling you to get help for your anger as meddling or uncaring, but as you learn and grow in this process you will eventually thank them for caring about your best interest and how you live in the world. People who care about you and want the best for you will have the courage to make suggestions for your success in life. Try not to have contempt prior to investigation.

Keep in mind that although anger is a normal human emotion, the way you choose to express your anger may not be normal or acceptable to those around you. Maybe you need to rethink your automatic responses toward people. Maybe you need to take more responsibility for your thoughts and actions than you have in the past. If you are not sure what you need to change at this point that's okay. The further you get into this program of change the more you will be finding out about your emotions and how you can experience and express them for a win-win situation.

The Best Part...

Anger does have a best part...the best part of anger and angry behavior is that you are in charge of it and you are in charge of your actions. You are the one with the power and authority to make powerful positive changes in your behavior and you are also the one with the power and authority to sit in your unhealthy behaviors. You *do* have choices in how you display your emotions.

One concept I want to share with you right from the start that I hear over and over from people who act out on their anger is that their bad behavior is "because of someone." "Someone pushed my buttons and caused me to react this way." "My actions are not my fault." "He made me, she made me." Hogwash! No one forces you into bad behavior just like no one can force you into learning healthy new behaviors. You are not a puppet on a string and no one is your puppeteer. Stop blaming and stop fooling yourself into thinking you are at someone else's mercy. You may have wounds or hurts in certain areas of your life, but still, no one has power over you to make you react in any way you don't want to react yourself. Take a few moments and really think about this concept. No one has the power to control your behavior even if it is old engrained behavior you have carried around for a lifetime. You can unlearn those old behaviors that get you into trouble over and over and replace them with healthy new behaviors. Remember: anger management isn't about eliminating anger from your list of emotions. It's about learning to manage your anger so it will work in positive ways in your life.

Isn't it refreshing to know that you have the power and authority to change your life? Can you become empowered just by reading this book or any other anger management book? No way! Can you just show up to anger management classes or skim a few pages in an online anger management class and poof your anger will be gone? Not a chance!

The work involved in behavioral change is strenuous and lengthy. Changing your behavior is some of the most difficult work you will ever do in your lifetime, but the payoffs are some of the best you will ever receive as a result of your hard work and effort. The goal in behavioral change is to start small and stay motivated. Open your mind, look around, understand yourself and your emotions better and look toward the future with positive regard. The past is the past, but the future is filled with your desires and possibilities. Contrary to what you might believe right now, personal happiness does not depend on life dealing you a good hand. How you respond to what comes your way will largely determine whether your life is fulfilling or not.

Wishcraft

Many people have told me over the years, "I have already taken anger management classes and it just doesn't seem to work for me." My questions to them are: What did you actually do to learn about your anger? What commitment have you made on a daily basis to look at your anger? What is your anger plan? I always count on the same ever popular blank stare and the same answer, "But I read everything I was supposed to read and it still just doesn't work for me."

Wouldn't it be nice if I could make a magic pill that would pop off this page and POOF!!…your angry behavior would be all better. Nothing is ever that easy, much less anger management.

I can't stress it enough. Changing your behavior requires patience, a lot of time, hard work and self examination. It also requires you to put what you are learning in this class into motion on a daily basis to make the changes you desire in your life. The words "anger management" will not make it happen for you. **You** make it happen. You are the catalyst in your own life. Get proactive in your life and get started in the process of change *today!*

Getting Started

Having the desire to implement positive changes in your life and starting the anger management process means you have made the realization that you are responsible for your life and are committed to change. It means that you have decided to become a person who lives in solution rather than a person living in the problem. You have realized that you are responsible for change and that this process is about you changing and not simply waiting for someone else to change so that your anger or bad feelings will go away.

People who live in solution know that the bad times will come and go, but also realize that you have a choice in how you handle your circumstances and how you manage your feelings. When you live in solution, you are proactive in your life and grow from your experiences rather than become a victim to your feelings. You know that your self worth comes from you and not your circumstances, surroundings or the people you encounter in your life.

Most importantly, you cannot give up in your struggle to change. Do not quit now that you have started the difficult process! Take baby steps in the process and don't let a minor set back create major defeat. Every day will not feel like a "winner" day in anger management. There will be slip ups and days when you feel like nothing you try is working. If you are even thinking about your life… it is working! Don't stop or quit now. The process is already in motion and you are on your way to making positive changes in your life.

Stages Of Change

Progressing through behavioral change is due to a combination of motivation, technique and dedication. Some of you will move quickly through the stages of change, while others will move more slowly and even take a step or two backward from time to time and that's okay. You are still growing and changing even in the times when you don't feel successful in your anger management quest.

The stages you will be going through in your anger management quest are: Awareness, Preparation, Action and Maintaining Gains.

Right now, at this stage of anger management you are in the **awareness stage** because you are seeking out information and reading this book. Awareness is about gathering information and seeing what fits into your life. Chapter 1 is all about awareness and as you read through the book you will begin to understand the importance awareness has in your life and the huge part it plays in anger management.

The **preparation stage** begins when you decide to actually make changes in your life and the way you express your anger. Preparation is about planning and studying. Preparation will happen in the upcoming chapters through work in your assignments and your journal.

The **action stage** happens when you start making real change in the way you live your life. While it is called the action stage I also like to refer to it as the living in solution stage. This is the stage when you will apply yourself to the changes and become very proactive in implementing changes in your life. You will actually be living the changes you decide to make in your life. The action stage is about having courage to implement change.

Maintaining gains is the stage when you accept that you are not perfect, that you will make mistakes and act inappropriately, but that you can recover from relapses in your behavior. Each time you lapse into old behaviors, you will be able to use the tools and strategies you have learned to pick yourself up and recover quickly. You will be able to move on and learn from your mistakes.

Where You Are Today

How many of you think you got where you are in your career or life in general by reading a book or manual and magically you became the person you are today? In order to become proficient in something I am sure you needed to practice certain skills to accomplish and perform your task well. A job, sports, art, career talents, college degree, motherhood, fatherhood, ... Anger management is no different than any other accomplishment in your life.

Take a moment now and think of something you had to struggle with in order to learn or think of an accomplishment that took hard work to achieve. Did the skill come quickly? Did it appear overnight? Did you need to practice to perfect your skill? Let's look at a few examples: Would you want a doctor who only reads how to perform your surgery or would you want one that actually practices his skill and is proficient at it? Would you want a barber who has actually had a pair of scissors in his hand or would you entrust your head to someone who looks at pictures in a book? Would you want a car mechanic who only read an article on how to change your spark plugs and swears he can do it even though he has never tried?

Important! I cannot stress it enough in this beginning stage of anger management. You must make a commitment to practice what you are reading and learning in this book on a daily basis. Put your plan into action! Get proactive in your life and begin living in solution rather than sitting in the problem. Reading alone will not gain you the success you desire in anger management. If you practice and put thought into what you are learning on a daily basis, not only will you become successful in managing your anger; it will be a valuable skill you will own for the rest of your life.

List some things you do well: (sports, career, computer games, cooking)

_____

_____

_____

List how long it took you to become good at the things you do well:

_____
_____
_____

What Should I Change?

You probably don't know what you need to change right now because you just started the anger management process and before you can make any change in your behavior, you need to know what to look for. How can you begin to look for the behaviors you need to change?

Becoming Aware

You **must** start paying attention to your behavior/anger on a daily basis. Old behaviors are like old habits. They become more and more comfortable and more automatic throughout your lifetime. Old behaviors are similar to that comfortable pair of old run over shoes you wear on Saturdays because they don't rub you the wrong way. However, it just might be the comfortable behaviors that are getting you into trouble. You need to pay attention and decide what changes you need to make in your own life. You are your own judge in this process.

Almost anyone you talk to, if they are being honest, would admit that they are comfortable in their old behaviors, good or bad, because they have been around for a very long time and they are familiar (comfortable). Who wants to put the hard work and effort into changing something that is comfortable and familiar to you?

Maybe the old behaviors make you feel safe and the only way you know how to cope with your emotions, but you have come to this program to make some changes and take some responsibilities. Making change is always a difficult process, especially in your behavior, but you have the power and control to make your life a more pleasant place to be by learning to manage your anger. Isn't that your goal?

The behaviors I would like to change are:

_____

_____

_____

Where Does It Come From?

Although everyone experiences anger in response to frustrating or abusive situations, most anger is generally short lived. No one is born with a chronic anger problem. Chronic anger and aggressive responses are learned.

Most people learn to express their anger when they are very young by modeling (observing) what they saw influential adults doing with their behavior. You basically observed how other people expressed anger and you copied their same behavior. Modeling for you might have happened by watching a parent, grandparents, an older sibling or maybe even a television personality.

Are you getting the idea that it might be a good chance to blame the parents or adults of your youth for your behavior? You might be right in coming to that conclusion, but remember that very few people are ever told how to react when they are angry. Unless people actually take the time to examine their behavior and make changes, the cycle continues and trickles down throughout families. You have an opportunity to break that cycle by the changes you are making in your life as an adult.

Children are usually not allowed to show anger in most households. As children or teenagers, how many of you were allowed to truly express your anger? How many of you had the luxury of looking your parents in the eye and telling them, "I'm really pissed off at you right now!"

If we are constantly told that we shouldn't experience something early in life, how are we supposed to deal with it as an adult? The chances are your parents probably learned how to not demonstrate anger or explosively show their anger from their parents and so right or wrong it becomes a genetic hand me down.

Wherever or however you learned your current angry behaviors, it took a long time for you to learn and become proficient in expressing them and the same is true when you are trying to relearn new ways to manage your anger. It will take time and energy, but you can do it. Let's not blame anymore. You are an adult now. You are not living with your childhood influences or in those familiar childhood surroundings. Take charge of your own behavior and be who you want to be in the world today. Remember, you have the power and authority to make it all happen. With hard work and effort you can become the adult you want to be in the world.

Eliminate Anger?

The goals of anger management are to reduce both your emotional feelings and the physiological arousal that anger causes, not to eliminate your anger. No one is ever wrong for feeling angry, but there are healthy and unhealthy ways you can use express your anger.
Learning to recognize and stop your behavior rather than explode in rage is a good start. We learned earlier, you probably won't be able to get rid of, or avoid the things or people

13

that enrage you, but you can learn to control your actions and behavior.

Just The Facts

I get asked this question over and over: What is anger and what causes it? There are no easy answers because anger can be triggered by many, many things or a combination of things and usually different for each of us. What may really anger me, may not even faze you. What causes you great anger and emotion may mean nothing to your spouse. Anger is not a black and white science. You might feel stressed out, you might be hungry, lonely, tired…Your anger depends on many different things in your life and only you hold the answer to the question. How do you get those difficult answers? You get the answers by self examination, paying attention and getting active in your process of change.

Anger is a natural and mostly automatic response to pain of one form or another. Anger can occur when you aren't feeling well, feel rejected, feel threatened, or experience a loss. Anger is often times described as a secondary emotion meaning something usually happens first to spark your emotions. In other words, anger is preceded by painful feelings. No one walks around angry all the time without some type of emotional or physical trigger.

Anger can also be considered a substitute emotion. By this I mean that sometimes people make themselves angry so that they don't have to feel pain. People change their feelings of pain into anger because it feels better to be angry than it does to be in pain. Some of you may use this technique and don't even realize you are doing it because it happens subconsciously. Others of you may be relating to anger as a substitute emotion and others are relating to being angry is much better than feeling emotional pain. Anger for some is power and it enables you to keep people away from you when you feel hurt.

Anger temporarily protects people from having to recognize and deal with their painful real feelings. Making yourself angry can help you to hide the reality that you find a situation frightening or that you feel vulnerable.

Fact:

- Anger is one of your emotions, along with happiness, sadness and fear.
- Anger is a completely normal, usually healthy emotion that varies in intensity from mild irritation to intense rage.
- Anger is a reaction to an inner emotion and not a planned action.
- Anger is considered a secondary emotion. Meaning, something usually triggers a bad thought or feeling and you begin to feel angry.
- Anger can also be caused by fear, stressful situations and fatigue.
- Worrying or brooding over personal problems or thoughts can cause anger.
- Repeated bad thoughts may increase your anger's intensity.
- Anger can be an instant reaction to a single event or it can be a response after numerous events

14

- Anger reduces stress and makes you feel temporarily powerful.
- Anger is a learned behavior. We imitate how others handled anger.

It's All Up To You

It's not the fact that you experience anger as an emotion that becomes a problem for you. It is how you choose to express your anger that can become a problem for you. What you do with your anger and how you display it is completely up to you. As you now understand, no one has magical powers over you to make you rant and rave, hit the dog, kick the car or act out viciously. You are the one totally responsible for your actions. You are the one who needs to look at yourself and change your own behavior.

Working through this book will help you to realize that you do have choices in how you display your anger.

Do We Ever Really Need Anger?

The answer is quiet simple, yes. Anger is a natural, adaptive response to threats; it inspires powerful, often aggressive, feelings and behaviors, which allows us to fight and defend ourselves when we are being attacked.

The natural instinctive way to express anger is to respond aggressively, making a certain amount of anger necessary for our survival. However, most of us are usually not under any kind of attack that would warrant aggression or anger to handle the situation. We may think we are under life threatening circumstances, but in most cases we really aren't being threatened. We are simply angry!

As negative as anger can be, it can also provoke you into making positive, powerful changes in your life. Let's look at an example of how anger can play a part in making a positive change in your life:

Michael

Michael came to work everyday to the same job he had for the past 15 years. While he liked his job, the boss made showing up for work more and more difficult every day. Most of the workers had very little respect for the boss and the way he managed his employees. He shoved more and more work on them to the point of causing exhaustion on a daily basis. Michael felt angry every day, every time he saw his boss and every time a new project was thrown his way. Night after night he came home to his family in a foul and irritated mood. He noticed that they too were paying the price for his anger.

One day Michael was tired of feeling angry and decided it was time for a change, to live in solution and become proactive in his life. Looking at the job openings in the human resources department, Michael noticed a new position in a different department. At first Michael felt he wasn't qualified for the job, but then he remembered the anger he felt every day and how his family was being affected. He applied, got the job and moved out of the old department. Anger propelled Michael out of an environment that had caused him grief and anger for 15 years. Anger can motivate great change. Yes, we need anger.

Emma

Emma felt angry every time a car whizzed by her house at 50 miles an hour in a 35 mile per hour zone. She felt frightened for the safety of her children and would yell angrily at the drivers every day to slow down. Day after day the cars would fly by her house while her children walked home from school on the sidewalks only a few feet away from the speeding cars. When her kids entered the house, Emma would be too overwhelmed with anger to talk about anything that happened in their day. Sensing her daily anger, the kids immediately went to their rooms after school to stay out of Emma's path even if they felt the need to talk with their mother. Emma knew her anger was getting stronger and she could see that her kids didn't enjoy coming home from school and being greeted in the same negative way day after day. Finally, Emma's anger got organized. She called other parents in the neighborhood to see if they noticed the speeding cars. Most of the parents were also angry and most shared in her frustration in the way drivers recklessly sped down the small street. Together they organized an active group of concerned parents who went before the City Council to explain their frustrations. After weeks of talks and planning, the City decided to strictly enforce the speed limit by posting more signs and assigning more police to canvass the area. The speeding problem slowly got resolved and Emma and the rest of the committee felt they had accomplished a huge solution in a very positive direction. Yes, we need anger to channel our passions and create change.

Grace

Grace experienced severe back pain as a result of a car accident years ago. Most times she had to depend on others to care for the house and even had to depend on others to help her physically. She felt angry at everyone because she felt helpless and she took much of her anger out on everyone around her. She ordered her husband and children around and made them feel terrible if they didn't perform to her liking. She would call them names such as lazy if her husband didn't jump right up to each of her demands. She told her children they wouldn't amount to anything because they could take care of the simplest of household duties. It was hard for Grace to feel good about herself; after all, she had to rely on everyone else to help her meet her own needs. Her anger made the situation worse not only for herself, but for her caretakers as well. The question to ask your self regarding Grace is this: is she entitled to have anger? If you have compassion for others you probably quickly answered, yes she is entitled to her anger and you would be right. Something happened to cause her anger. Remember, anger is a secondary emotion. It could be an incident such as Grace's, or it could your own repetitive thinking or low self esteem that can start the anger circle in motion. While Grace has the right to "feel' the emotion of anger, does she have a right to treat others the way she treats her family? Do you think Grace needs an anger plan to help her understand her feelings of helplessness? As you can see, anger comes from many different emotions and areas in life. While anger might feel justified in the moment you still have a responsibility to understand your underlying emotions and then start the process of finding solutions to manage your emotions.

Max

Max is a 16 year old junior in high school who struck a deal with his parents. His parents would pay for gas, clothing, and give him money for activities however there were strings attached. If he was successful in school and brought home good grades, if he didn't drink and if he met his curfews he had no problems. If, however he talked back to his parents, brought home poor grades or disregarded the house hold rules the gas, clothing and spending money would be yanked out from under him. This type of agreement made Max feel compromised and it made him angry. He felt as though he had to toe the line in order to get what he feels he deserves. Even though there is no injustice here Max did experience anger. He felt compromised. If you give us this, we will give you that. Is his anger justified? You could probably think of a time when you were in this type of situation and felt an uneasy angry feeling. It is how you break it down and think about it that could make all the difference to your emotions. Max did eventually think about his situation and he realized that he was getting a pretty good deal. He is still living under his parent's roof so it was their rules he needs to live by any way. What was expected of him was no different than what was expected of his friends in their households. While Max might not have liked the give and take (mostly the give) he was able to rationalize his anger and come to an understanding that he could have anger and be okay, but he could also get past it by rationalizing the facts of the situation.

The Beginning Phase

Find a notebook you can use to make an anger journal. In the journal, I want you to start off with a contract to yourself. The contract states that you are going to try to calm your anger for a twenty-four hour period. Make your contract look like this:

I _____ between _____ & _____ on (date) _____ promise to attempt to remain calm and to act in a non-aggressive manner.

_____

Your Signature

While I'm sure you understand this is a contract only to yourself and by yourself, I want you to think of it as a legally binding contract. It is the beginning phase of making a commitment to calm your anger, recognizing and admitting that you have a problem with anger. Begin to honor yourself in this process by honoring your contract. You are probably asking what should I do during this twenty-four hour period until I learn how to manage my anger?

Recognize and admit that you feel angry. Remember, feeling angry is okay.

Try not to turn your anger into a behavior (yell, scream, hit).

Let the anger come and go, but do not dwell on it. Do not keep re-hatching the anger or your trigger thoughts over and over again. If the trigger thoughts keep repeating over and over try to stop or turn the negative thought into a positive thought. Example: I hate that I have to take this anger management class. Turn the thought around: I might not like that I have to take this class, but I am going to learn new techniques to change my life. Or, think of a pleasant event or something that makes you happy, but do not allow yourself to dwell on the same bad thoughts. Consider taking up a physical activity such as taking a walk around the block, exercise, bike riding, yoga… Get active.

In the process of teaching this program, many people have told me they are unable to extend themselves for a full 24 hour period especially in the beginning. That's okay. Like we talked earlier in this chapter, anger management is a process of building strength in small amounts similar to taking baby steps. If you can't make a 24 hour contract, make it a 12 hour contract and if you can't make a 12 hour contract, make it a one hour contract. This anger management program is about designing techniques which are right for your life and suit your individual needs. You know what you can handle. If you can make it for a full hour, congratulate yourself and extend it for another hour. Real change happens gradually.

Reward yourself when you fulfill your contract. A simple, healthy reward will sometimes help you to stay on track.

What else can I do during this 24-hour period? During this 24-hour period, start becoming aware of and paying attention to what makes you angry or uneasy. One of the best ways to help you keep track of your angry behaviors is by writing them down in a journal.

Journaling

Before you frown and think that there is no point in writing all this stuff down and that it is way too much work, let me tell you that in order for you to learn about yourself and understand why you get angry you need to study yourself and your behavior. Writing it down will allow you to go back and review your anger at a time when you are more clear-headed and ready to examine your behaviors. You can't always stop to analyze yourself when you are in the heat of a feeling, but you can put thought into your behaviors when you are calm and ready to think rationally.

Journaling in this process is a MUST!! A journal is a safe place where you can let your feelings out and review them at a time when you are calm and ready to learn about yourself. Journaling is an extremely profound tool in getting to know yourself better and organizing your changes. The journal is probably one of the most valuable tools you will use in this class and if you are skeptical I challenge you to try it and see for yourself.

Your journal should contain the following:

- Write down the time and where you were angry.
- What you did when you became angry. What behaviors did you experience while you were angry?
- Consequences of your angry behavior. Did it cost you something?
- Did you do anything to try to stop your angry behaviors? Is so, what did you do and why?

Example journal entry:

Time: 9:30 AM

Where you became angry: At work.

What you did: Started throwing things around on my desk.

Consequences: Co-workers stayed away from me for the rest of the day. I could sense they were afraid to approach me.

What I did to stop angry behavior: Took a few deep breathes and told myself it wasn't really that bad. Thought about the movie I saw last night.

Why I used this method: I couldn't leave work and I needed a quick fix.

If you want to make the process easier, you might copy this blank form and fill it in whenever you feel angry. I want to make this process as easy as possible so that you have staying power!

Time: _____

Where you became angry: _____

What you did: _____

Consequences: _____

What I did to stop my angry behavior:

_____

Why I used this method: _____

This is another example of an anger management self monitoring form. You might design a form of your own that works better for you.

SELF MONITORING FORM

TRIGGER: What happened that started your anger?

_____
_____
_____

WHAT HAPPENED INSIDE? What was the angry episode like for you? What did you think about? How did you feel physically? What did you do with your anger?

I thought:

_____
_____
_____

I physically felt:

_____
_____
_____

What I did with my anger:

_____
_____
_____

WHAT HAPPENED OUTSIDE? How did you display your anger? What did others tell you about your anger?

_____
_____
_____

THE END: How did the episode end? What happened? If the anger was directed at another person; what is your relationship like with that person now? Was the anger harmful or helpful?

_____
_____
_____

The main point of the journal is to "get it all out on paper" and then go back later or the next day and try to understand and make sense of your emotions. The point is to put the anger event in perspective when you are in a relaxed state of being and able to think rationally. When you take the time to write about and review your anger episode you are more likely to understand why you became angry. You may even attach a few other emotions as culprits to your anger. Maybe you will determine that you weren't angry at all, but you acted out your emotions in an old familiar behavior. There are many, many reasons for acting out your emotions and journaling is one of the best ways to help you understand yourself better. Journaling is a must in anger management. Don't skip this step of the process. It is the very first layer of the strong foundation we are building for behavioral change.

One common criticism I often heard people say is that they can't carry a journal with them wherever they go or they don't always have an opportunity to write when they are angry. You don't have to whip out a piece of paper and pencil when you are in the heat of your anger, but try to write in your journal very soon after you experience your angry event. Even if nothing angers you on a particular day, I want you to write about your feelings. Journaling isn't "all" about recording the negative events happening to you. What went **right** for you in your day? What techniques made you feel successful? Journaling is also about recording your successes, happiness and the progress you are making in your journey of change.

Commitment Is A Powerful Tool For Change

We already talked about the stages of change and I now want to introduce you to commitment which is another very important tool in behavioral change. If you want to make powerful changes in your life, you must decide to make the changes you desire and stay committed to your process.

Making a commitment early on in the program is a step in a positive direction and gives you positive feelings about yourself. It keeps you on the roller coaster of life. With all the ups and downs, successes and failures you will feel in your process of anger management, a commitment keeps you holding on knowing that you can continue on your path no matter how rough the journey can get: *you are committed to your process*.

Commitment to behavioral change is a very important and necessary step. Without commitment, this whole process will only be more difficult for you and you probably won't be very successful in making the changes you desire. Along with awareness, commitment is one of the first steps in the process of anger management. A commitment brings you closer to the life you want tomorrow today.

I, _____ am committed to making the changes I desire in my life and working toward my goal of controlling anger by learning and growing in the process.

Keep in mind that following your anger management treatment plan is no different than following any other treatment plan you may have used in your life. For example, if you want to lose weight you follow a diet plan and you exercise. You won't see results if you don't put your plan into action. If you suffer from a health condition, you follow your treatment plan to maintain proper health. Behavioral change programs are no different than any other treatment plan. In order to become successful you have to work on the assignments and make a pledge to be diligent in your work. To become successful you MUST make the time to get healthy. The process of learning about how to change your behavior and understanding your emotions is about you uncovering some difficult past behaviors and then switching over to living in the present. No one said this was going to be easy, but I guarantee you it will be rewarding!

Assignment For The Week

Take a full week to practice and understand this chapter. Put thought into each assignment and work slowly through the chapter. It is better that you understand the material than it is to simply finish it quickly and without effort. You are laying the foundation in anger management and you must have a first layer and a good understanding of the material to move into higher levels of this program. Even though some of this first chapter seems like common sense, a commitment to change requires deep thought and energy to move forward in a new future. Take your time. Get committed in your process of change

Start your change by implementing the 24-hour commitment contract. Will there be times in these beginning stages that you break your contract? Sure. You are just learning how to manage and control something that has been a part of your life for a very long time.

Slipping up is acceptable, but only if you try harder the next time. You must stay committed to the process of anger management.

Keep your journal all week. Try to carry your journal with you and every time you feel angry, write it down. If you can't write in the heat of the moment, write in your journal when you are calm. Try to recall the events that caused your anger. You will get to know your anger and yourself much better during this important process.

Think about the following questions:

What causes your anger?

Why are you taking anger management?

What are your goals in anger management?

What price have you paid to display your angry behavior?

How can I stay positive and motivated in anger management?

Key Point: Working on problematic behavior isn't easy by any means, but you are already 50% ahead of the game just by admitting that you could use some help in learning to handle your anger.

Key Point: In order for real behavioral change to take place, the anger management techniques you practice must be "right" for you and your life. The techniques and solutions need to come from self investigations of your life and your own frame of reference. Self investigations require you focus on your behavior and emotions. Focusing on your self, believe it or not, is tough work. We forget about ourselves in the busy paces of life, but this is about behavioral change. You have to change out of the mode of automatic pilot and just doing the familiar behavior to first captain in the driver's seat of your own life.

Key Point: If you aren't willing to do your share of work in this program, you probably won't be very successful in anger management. That statement isn't meant to discourage you in your process of change, but to inform you that the work we do here is difficult. To make the changes you want to make in your life takes hard work and dedication. I can coach you along in the process and provide information, but the changes you desire come from you implementing the program ideas into your life and finding solutions that are right for your life.

Key Point: Changing your behavior is some of the toughest work you will do in your lifetime, but I have no doubt that you can do it. I have seen thousands of people change their lives with the right tools for success. The main thing you need to keep in mind is that anger management is not about punishing you. Anger management is about finding solutions so that you can live the life you deserve. Whatever brought you to this point in your life in seeking out help for anger management is in the past. It is where you go from here that counts.

In up coming chapters we are going to be talking about living in solutions rather than living in problems and living positively rather than living negatively. Let's start practicing looking for the good early in the process. Take a moment now and write about some of the good things in your life. What good things happened to you during the week? What did you like about your week/day? What worked for you today? What do you like about your life? What do you like about yourself?

It is going to take energy to make the positive changes that you desire in your behavior, but it will be well worth the effort when you see changes working in your life. The average person will make many important investments in their lifetime, but none as important as learning healthy new behaviors to replace the ones that aren't working. It is the deal you have been looking for!

I have no doubt that you can successfully manage your anger, but you have to first understand your emotions. In order to understand your emotions you need to pay attention to yourself (awareness) and you must take time to put yourself first on our journey of learning anger management.

Chapter 2

Reading The Signs

Review

- Anger is a normal emotion and usually secondary to other bad feelings or thoughts.
- A 24 hour contract is a commitment to yourself to calm your anger for a 24 hour period or less.
- The purpose of anger management is to reduce both your emotional feelings and the physiological arousal that anger causes, not to eliminate your anger completely.
- You have choices when you experience anger. You can act out in bad behavior or you can chose to manage your emotions.
- Anger is needed for emergency or life threatening situations.
- Anger can produce positive changes.
- Realizing that you have anger is the first step in learning to manage it and is the foundation of anger management.

The main focus of Chapter 2 is going to be keeping you focused on and recognizing your behavior. At first you might feel uncomfortable with all the life transformation talk and assignments and you might feel as though you are stepping out of your comfort zone and taking on an uncomfortable new role in your life. That's good! It's normal to feel uncomfortable with change. You have to step outside the comfort zone to make real and lasting change in your life. There will always be some degree of discomfort in making big changes in your life. You will be okay in your process of change. Staying strong and staying motivated are key issues right now. You **can** do this!

Let's take a few minutes before we start Chapter 2 to talk about some issues that may have come up for you this past week or in Chapter 1.

One of the biggest issues that usually surfaces in Chapter 1 is if you are really experiencing anger or is it another emotion that is causing you difficulty? Are people seeing me accurately? I don't feel angry…. Do I? Am I really angry?

As you now know, anger is a very complicated emotion and maybe you are not sure if you are experiencing anger at this point or not. Let me help to guide you in finding some of the answers.

I think you have a problem with anger if:

You hurt others with your anger.

You never get angry.

You allow others to hurt you with their anger.

You hurt yourself with your anger.

You are afraid to express your anger.

You hold onto your anger and are unable to forgive and forget.

You find sneaky ways of getting back at people.

You cannot express your anger directly.

You are angry a good deal of the time.

You are out of control when it comes to your anger.

You are negative, critical, blaming.

You feel helpless and hopeless against your anger.

Your way of expressing anger is jeopardizing your job or family relationships.

You don't know why you respond with anger.

You take your anger out on innocent people.

Your anger is eating you up inside.

You involve yourself with other angry or violent people.

You allow yourself to be emotionally or physically abused by others.

Do your see yourself in any of those statements? Most people are probably answering yes to some of the statements. Some of you might be answering yes to most of the statements and there will be some of you who aren't sure. It's okay to be unsure at this point in the program because you are in the beginning stages of learning anger management. Being unsure is fine. Being unsure means you are open to exploration and finding new ways of living your life in positive solution. On the other hand, being in denial about your behavior is not going to change your behavior. It is going to keep you locked into old, unsuccessful ways of managing your emotions. Staying in denial is going to keep you in that uncomfortable rut you are trying to get yourself out of. Be open to possibilities and change will come.

I personally think if we are being honest with ourselves we have all handled our anger in ways that really wasn't in our best interest or the best interest of our loved ones from time to time. After all, we are human and part of being human is making mistakes along the way, but we also have a responsibility in being an adult and that is to recognize our short comings and find positive ways to live in solution. Having short comings is not the problem. Not addressing the shortcomings is the problem. We can't just hurt ourselves or others and walk away without taking responsibility. Not taking responsibility for your behavior doesn't work in any facet of your life. Part of being an adult means taking responsibility for your life and your behavior.

Another common issue that comes up in the first week is people asking themselves if they are doing "okay" in this process. If you are even thinking about yourself... you are doing great! Are you committed to change? Then you are right on target. If you are coming up with answers for your behavior or emotions you are doing fantastic!

An even bigger issue that usually comes up after the first chapter is who do I include in my process of change? Who should I talk with about my anger management process? Is it good idea to discuss things with relatives or friends? That's a tough question to answer and you will need to be your own best judge on this decision. What I can tell you, and you already know this from Chapter 1, is that I stress this process is about you. It isn't about answering to someone else or managing your anger according to what someone else wants you to do. I am trying to get you to think for yourself about your own life and what you need and want to transform for yourself. You have to answer to yourself in your process of change and I don't recommend reporting in to someone who isn't in your corner of change. However, if you feel comfortable sharing your process with a significant person in your life that you are making change I support your decision if that person is supportive and not criticizing your work or undermining your progress. If your family is behind you all the way, include them in your process. I have some people who include their whole family in the process because they want to make this process work in their family dynamic. That's great! There is no better way to learn something than to teach it yourself. Others will learn and grow from the example you set and you can be a huge catalyst for change.

You might also consider sharing your process face to face with a counselor or therapist in your area. A counselor or therapist is always an advocate for positive change and if you feel as though you are going this process alone, please seek out help in your local area. There are some suggestions on where to look for a competent therapist in the back of this book. Remember, reaching out for help is not a sign of weakness. It is a sign of strength. You might also consider visiting the peer-to-peer discussion group on

AngerManagementOnline.com for moral support. The people on AngerManagementOnline.com are people just like you working hard to find the answers to their anger and how to live in solution.

After a week or two of anger management some people have brought up the fact that certain friends and family members are making it hard for them to make changes in their lives. Believe it or not, there are family members or friends out there who encourage you to change and when you do make changes might not like it. I know that is a confusing message, but it does happen. During your process of change you get stronger and you get more confident and you might change in areas that people won't like. That's okay. Remember, this is a process about you and what makes you feel good about your own life. Behavioral change sometimes does rock the boat, but you need to stay strong, stay with your process and things will eventually smooth out.

Something else that usually surfaces from Chapter 1 is confusion over hearing that anger can be considered healthy and most people want more clarification on healthy anger.

The best way for me to describe healthy anger is this:

Anger is a tricky emotion and difficult to consider normal until you understand it better and learn how to use it in healthy ways. People who use anger in a healthy manner have a normal relationship with their anger. They think of anger as a normal part of life, that anger is a signal of something wrong, but doesn't necessarily require immediate reaction in every situation. Healthy anger is monitored and doesn't just happen automatically without your knowledge. Healthy anger is expressed in moderation so that you don't have to lose control to get your point across. The goal in experiencing anger is to solve problems, not just lash out in uncontrolled behavior. Healthy anger is stated in a way that others can understand it. Once an issue is solved anger is relinquished and you move on in your day.

Reviewing Your Journal

Remember we talked in Chapter One about the stages of changes and that the first stage is awareness. If you are working the steps in Chapter One you are already mastering the awareness stage of change. Journaling is the preparation stage in change. Journaling will help you to identify and become aware of your anger triggers and will give you some insight into how proportional your angry outbursts are to the various situations that provoke them. The more you learn about your personal anger triggers, the better your chances of success in changing how you express anger.

Now let's take a look at your journal.

In reviewing your journal from this past week, what are you learning about yourself and your behavior? Are you starting to see any patterns in your anger such as: the time of day you notice your anger, where is your anger happening, when do you notice your anger or why did you feel angry? Are you noticing events or circumstances that trigger your anger or bad feelings such as: location, work, or a particular person? Having a good understanding of when, where, why and how intensely you feel anger will aid in pin pointing situations that you may need to avoid in the future or change in order to keep your anger at a milder or more manageable level.

As you are learning, the main purpose of writing in your journal is for you to start paying attention to yourself and your emotions. Journaling also helps you to become more proactive in the process of behavioral change by making you an active participant. If you don't take the time to understand your emotions you will be missing out on a very important step of anger management. Journaling also serves as a means of getting your emotions, feelings and frustrations out on paper so that you can examine your reactions objectively and have a better understanding of yourself when you are calm and ready to do your work in self reflection.

Writing in your journal is not only answer producing, but it should also feel like a major relief to you because you can get your emotions out in a safe environment without feeling judged by others. You will be surprised how great it is going to feel and how much there is to gain in writing about your feelings. The second benefit of writing in your journal is reviewing your entries when you are in a calm mood. Being in a calm mood will enable you to think about your journal entries with your rational brain. Ask yourself questions in your journal: What happened to cause my anger? How could I have done things differently? What if this situation happens to me again? What will I do in the future when a similar situation arises?

Putting the pieces of the puzzle together by reviewing your journal when you are in a calm mood will help you to understand and avoid the things that escalate your anger out of control. What you write in your journal will reveal how you were thinking in the heat of your anger. Your journal entries will also help you to realize that your emotions may not have been exactly on target when you were feeling angry. You may think you were angry in a given situation when really on closer inspection you might have been feeling fear, surprise, guilt or shame etc. We will get into more emotions that can mask themselves as anger later, but just be aware in this beginning phase that there are other emotions that can be mistaken for anger. Reviewing your journal will help to paint a clearer picture of your emotions. Journaling allows you the chance to examine your thoughts and feelings and at the same time guide you into learning your necessary changes for anger control.

As you examine the entries in your journal, try to remember how intensely (strong) you felt your anger (or emotion) and how you acted out on your feelings.

Did you act out your anger or did you keep it inside?

Did you feel uneasy like you wanted to explode, but thought it would be better to keep a lid on it and let it boil inside?

How long did your anger last?

Were you able to move on from your anger quickly or did it linger and ruin your day?

Do you think your anger episode was mild, moderate or strong?

We have all heard the old saying, "Prevention is the best medicine." Being able to predict what situations will provoke you will be a tremendous aid in helping you keep your anger under control. You can choose to avoid provoking situations entirely, or, if that isn't possible, you can prepare yourself with ways to minimize the danger of your losing control prior to entering your trigger situations.

Remember, the purpose of your journal is to help you identify patterns of behavior and specific recurring situations that really "push your buttons." The more accurately you observe your feelings and behaviors the more detailed your journal, the more likely you will be able to identify your triggers and how you react to those triggers. Understanding the ways in which you experience anger can help you plan strategies to cope with your emotions in more productive ways. Once you have identified your triggers and begin to understand them, you will be able to work more constructively to control your responses to those triggers. Be aware that anger triggering thoughts occur automatically and almost instantaneously, so it will take some conscious work on your part to identify them. Remember the awareness stage we discussed in Chapter One?

A key point to watch out for when you are journaling is when you start to justify your anger. When you feel justified in your anger; you are giving yourself permission to feel angry whether or not it makes sense for you to feel that way. While experiencing anger is okay, it does not mean that choosing to act on your angry feelings is always justified. Be open to gaining a new or different perspective on your situation and don't hold on so tightly to being "right."

As you are reviewing your journal and learning about your triggers pay attention to:

What happened that made you feel pain or feel stressed out?

What thoughts were going through your mind?

What was the effect of your behavior on your or on others?

What did you actually do?

How did you feel in the heat of the moment and how did you feel after the episode, how did you feel a few days after the event?

What were the consequences of the incident?

Next week as you continue in your journal I would like to add on that you pay attention to recurring themes or triggers that bring on your anger. Begin to notice if your anger triggering thoughts are reoccurring and begin tracking your thought patterns to look for common themes in your experiences. What we are really looking for are circumstances or situations that really push your buttons. The more accurately you can observe your feelings and behaviors, the more likely you will be able to identify your anger triggers and how you react to them. Understanding the ways in which you experience anger can help you plan strategies to cope with your emotions in more productive ways.

Don't Just Write It, Rate It

One of the most important things you need to know about your anger is what actually triggers it and the second most important thing you need to know about your anger is how intensely you *feel* or experience it. I am going to add an additional assignment to writing in the journal called rating your anger.

Putting your anger into categories or rating it by intensity (mild, moderate and strong), will aid you in learning how strong your anger can get during an anger episode. The intensity of your anger could serve as a gauge of how you might act out physically when you feel angry. For example: mild anger is usually fairly tolerable or an annoyance that can be easily dealt with. In contrast, if you are feeling strong anger it is not as tolerable and you may feel the need to act out or release the uncomfortable feelings and wind up regretting it later.

Making yourself aware of the intensity of your anger will help you avoid situations that put you at the greatest risk of uncontrolled anger. The goal is not to set yourself up for failure by putting yourself in surroundings that you already learned from writing in your journal causes you to have strong anger. The goal of rating your anger is to get you in a planning mode for situations you determine make you feel angry and live in a solution rather than living in the problem. For example, if waiting in long lines puts your anger at a strong level, don't plan on going to the movies on Friday night or Saturday afternoon. If traffic jams on the freeway make your anger intolerable and uncontrollable, don't make plans to meet someone at 6 P.M. Friday night. If you hate to read, don't sign up for a book club because your best friend talks you into it. Planning is not running away. Planning is living in solution.

How Rating Works And The Benefits

Have you ever tried to explain a physical or emotional feeling to someone else and you're not quiet sure how to let them know exactly how you are feeling? For example, have you ever experienced some type of pain and you wanted to let someone else know how badly you feel the pain? Or, have you ever had a strong anger episode and wanted to describe the intensity to someone else? How can you possibly describe a pain or feeling to someone else that only you are experiencing? Maybe you've gone to the doctor or hospital for an ache or pain and you have been asked how strongly you felt the pain. How can you explain what you are feeling to someone else?

For example, let's say you had a headache and you went to the doctor for help in managing the pain. The doctor may ask you how intensely you feel the pain on a scale from 1-10. If a rating of 1 was barely any pain and 10 was excruciating pain, how would you describe the pain?

What you are really doing is rating how intensely you feel the pain. While you are in pain, just like when you are angry, the question may seem irritating, but the purpose for the rating question is very real. The doctor needs to know what plan of action to take in making you feel comfortable.

Let's say you told your doctor that your pain was a 2 on the scale from 1-10. He may tell you to use some ice and lie down in a quite room for awhile until the pain goes away. However, if you told your doctor that your pain was a 10 on the same scale the treatment plan would probably be much different. It would require further examination, more testing and observation, just like your strong anger. Anger at a rating of 1 on the scale from 1-10 is an annoyance, an anger rating of a 5 is frustrating and stressful, but an anger rating of 10 requires you to take immediate action!

Rating Your Anger

Why do I encourage applying a rating scale to anger management? Again, rating your anger will help you understand how intensely you feel your anger in many different situations. Just like the doctor, you are going to decide the amount of attention your anger requires. The whole process of rating your anger is designed to get you proactive in the process of anger management by letting you be the judge of your anger.

Anger ratings are also important because they provide valuable feedback about how likely you are to lose control or explode at any given moment. By training yourself to recognize when you are getting increasingly angry, you will improve your chances of being able to maintain control by taking steps to reverse the increasing anger. While anger ratings help you to become conscious of your anger, they won't help you stop being angry. It is your job to become aware of your emotions and then move into a healthy solution.

If your anger is a 1-2, you are probably noticing it, you are aware and monitoring it. You realize it's an annoyance, but you are also paying attention and have caught yourself having some bad feelings. This is the point when anger management techniques can be the most successfully utilized.

If your anger is a 5-6, you hopefully realize that you need to be more aware because your anger is moderately strong and could escalate without your conscious attention. You are able to identify your anger quickly, maybe even express it in a raised voice. Anger management techniques are still successful with moderate anger, but you need to move quickly into resolution or your anger may escalate to stronger levels much faster than at a lower level.

If your anger is a 9-10, it should be clear that you definitely need to pay attention to your behavior. Unattended strong anger can make you act out physically and uncontrollably. The goal in rating anger is to not allow your anger to reach a strong of intensity, but rather to put resolution on your anger before it reaches this stage. The real challenge in the rating game is to catch your anger at a mild level so that you can move immediately into solution. Take the challenge and resolve your anger at an annoyance level rather than turning your actions into regret simply because you didn't pay attention to your warning signs.

By writing in your journal and becoming familiar with your anger intensity, you will begin to recognize your anger before you act out in destructive ways. You must learn to recognize the signs and intensity of your anger. You must become proficient in reading your signs quickly and accurately so that your actions will match the emotion.

Try It

Now you are going to rate your anger on a scale from 1-10. 1 is considered mild anger, 5 would be moderate anger and 10 is strong anger. Draw the scale in your journal so it is easier for you to envision.

Mild Anger			Moderate Anger				Very Angry		
1	2	3	4	5	6	7	8	9	10

Are there any other words you could use on your scale to describe your anger? Be creative. Have some fun with this and come up with words you might use to describe your anger. Draw several scales in your journal and label them.

1	2	3	4	5	6	7	8	9	10
	Minimal			Moderate				Severe	

1	2	3	4	5	6	7	8	9	10
	Relaxed			Irritated				Pissed off	

1	2	3	4	5	6	7	8	9	10
	Home			Work				Traffic	

Mild, Moderate or Strong

To help you decide if your anger is mild, moderate or strong look at some examples of what anger at all stages might look like:

Your anger might be weak to mild if you feel frustrated when annoying situations occur.

Examples of **mild** anger may be:

- Your anger only lasts a few minutes.
- Your body stays calm; you are not taking the situation very seriously.
- Words to describe weak or mild anger could be: annoyed, irritated, and frustrated.

You may have a **moderate** amount of anger if:

- You identify anger when you feel it and it is gone after you express it.
- You feel like you need to raise your voice.
- Your body feels tense, but recovers in a short time to a calm state.
- You might say you are mad or pissed off.

You may have a **strong** amount of anger if:

- Your whole body is out of control, you feel like you are going to explode, unable to sit, to think clearly.
- You want to attack others.
- You feel like you are in danger.
- It takes more than a few hours or days to recover.
- You say you are furious, boiling, enraged.

Andrea Rates Her Anger

Andrea and Seth haven't seen much of each other lately. It seems that Seth has been putting in a lot of hours at work because he knows that at the end of the month there could be a huge promotion in the department. Andrea is juggling her life too. She has been working part-time and trying to finish her college degree. They both agree they miss spending time together, but they also know they both need to work hard right now to get where they want to be in life. Andrea and Seth made an agreement on Friday nights; they will quit working and studying early to be together for the entire evening. They both agree to be home at 5:30 p.m. for dinner and a movie.

Andrea kept her end of the bargain by coming home early to be with Seth and make a nice dinner for the two of them. When seven o'clock rolls around, it is pretty clear to Andrea that Seth is backing out on their agreement. Andrea tries to call Seth at work only to find out he hasn't been there since 6:00 p.m. Finally, at 8:30 PM, Seth strolled through the door with a huge smile on his face. Seems he had dinner with the boss because he wanted to present some ideas he had for a new project he was working on.

Andrea was relieved to see Seth, but her anger quickly reached the boiling point. She tried very hard to keep it inside because she could see the excitement and passion on Seth's face, but she could no longer stuff her feelings. With one quick throw, she hurled the phone at Seth barely missing his head and making a hole in the wall. She remembers yelling at the time, "Have you ever heard of a phone you idiot?"

Andrea's Journal

Time: 8:30 PM Friday

Where: Home

What I did: Threw the phone at my husband because he was over 3 hours late and never bothered to call me. Inconsiderate!

Consequences: My husband isn't speaking to me. I made a hole in the wall from throwing the phone and it will be expensive to repair. We don't have the extra money.

Strategies: I tried to remain calm and not let my feelings out, but I was really angry that Seth could care less about me. That's what it felt like to me.

Reason for Strategy: I thought that if I kept my feelings inside, my husband wouldn't know how badly he hurt me by not bothering to pick up the phone to call me. I felt out of control.

Intensity: 10!! Strong!!

Would you agree with Andrea's intensity? Did she have a right to be angry? Did she have the right to become physical and throw things risking harm to both of them or call him names? How do you think Andrea should have handled the situation? How would you do things differently?

Doris Rates Her Anger

Doris was looking forward to a date she had planned with Oliver for the past 2 weeks. It seemed like Oliver would never ask her out, but one day to her great surprise, Oliver got the courage to ask Doris on a date. Explaining that he was never really very good at making plans, he asked Doris to plan the evening any way she wanted and he would be happy to oblige. For 2 weeks Doris planned the perfect date, a movie she couldn't wait to see and dinner at her favorite restaurant. It seemed like a dream come true for Doris.

It was date night around 6 p.m. when the phone rang. It was Oliver apologizing that he would not be able to go on the long anticipated date because he was called in to work. Instantly, Doris felt angry because she planned for two weeks for this special night. Why did he have to go into work on this night? Was he trying to get out of the date?

Oliver explained to Doris that although they could not go on this date, he very much wanted to go out with her. He also explained that there was no one to cover this shift and that his boss was frantically calling everyone in the department to see who could help out. Oliver felt obligated to take the shift because his boss always allowed him to have time off when he needed for other activities. Oliver apologized to Doris for ruining her night and promised to make it up to her very soon.

After hanging up the phone, Doris realized that she was angry, but she also knew that Oliver really had no choice in the matter. She actually admired his strong work ethic and trusted that he would take her out soon. It was part of her attraction to Oliver in the first place. She gave her friend Amy a call to see if she could go to the movie instead of staying home. Amy was happy to get the invitation and although it was not the perfect night for Doris she was able to make the best of it and live in solution.

Time: 6 PM Saturday

Where: Home

What I did: Felt angry because my night with Oliver was canceled at the last minute after 2 weeks of planning.

Consequences: Realized that I needed to make a different plan for the night if I wanted to go out.

Strategy: Called my friend Amy. Went to a movie and out to dinner.

Reason for Strategy: I didn't want to stay home and think about not going out with Oliver. I wanted to go out, have a good time and get my mind off not seeing Oliver.

Intensity: 2

Would you agree with her intensity? Did she have the right to be hurt or angry? Were her actions appropriate for the situation? Instead of dwelling on the problem, Doris made an alternative plan to live in solution rather than disappointment. Are there any other emotions that Doris may have felt other than anger? Disappointed? Frustrated? Hurt?

Andrew Rates His Anger

Andrew had an appointment with his doctor at 11:30. Andrew is an extremely impatient person; he hates to wait for anyone! He arrived at the office at 11:15 to find it standing room only and filled with sick patients. When 12:00 came, Andrew was still in the waiting room. He could feel his whole body start to tense up and his heart began to race.

At 12:15, he asked the office girl when she thought the doctor might be seeing him. The office girl curtly told him that the way the doctor sees his patients is out of her control and for him to just be patient.

Finally at 12:30, Andrew had had it. People where coughing all over him, no where to sit down and not a decent magazine in the place! He again approached the office girl and yelled, "What an idiot you are to have an office full of people and only one doctor!" "I'm leaving now because I can't wait any longer and you can forget about me ever coming back here!"

Andrew left the office and drove back to work. On his way back, he listened to the radio and made a few phone calls. When he got back to work, his co-worker Michael asked him what he found out at the doctors office. In a calm voice he told Michael, "Nothing today, couldn't fit me in."

Time: 11:30 A.M.

Where: Doctor's office

What I did: Yelled at the office girl and told her she was an idiot.

Consequences: I would feel foolish ever going back there again. Now I have to find a different doctor. The office staff is not responsible for the doctor.

Strategies: I looked for a magazine, but there weren't any good ones there.

Reason for Strategy: If I had something to read or look at I might have been able to keep my cool.

Intensity: 7 I was over it after I got out of there.

Your Turn

Time: _____

Where: _____

What I did: _____

Consequences: _____

_____

Strategies: _____

_____

Reason for strategy: _____

_____

_____

Intensity: _____

What Can I Do Differently Right Now?

Begin to look for clues of your anger by reviewing your journal entries for patterns of your behavior on a daily basis and then come up with solutions to the problem. For example, if you see a pattern in your anger when you are stuck in traffic driving to work, try to make a plan to change what you are doing. Ask yourself: is there a different route I can take or can I leave at a different time? Can I change my hours at work to avoid heavy traffic back up?

What if you are unable to make any of these changes? What if your hours of work must stay the same or there is only one route you can take to your destination? Think about other ways to combat your anger rather than stay victim to your feelings. Try some books on tape, listen to your favorite music, find a new radio station, practice relaxation techniques or leave earlier so that you can take your time getting to your destination. You need to take control, be creative and make a plan that keeps you moving successfully in managing your anger. Remember, anger management is about being proactive in solution, not sitting in the problem.

What if you notice your anger is a 10 at the market standing in long lines? Be creative! Think: Is there a different time to go to the market that is less crowded? Can I make fewer trips to the market if I stock up on things now? Is there a different store that is less crowded? Is there an affordable grocery delivery service in my area?

Take charge of your anger by thinking of solutions that will put you in control of your life. Try not to think of changing your routine as a hassle; rather, think of change as a strategy in your self improvement plan. Sometimes you may simply need to give yourself options to manage your anger. Think creatively! Don't be a victim to your anger.

Don't be a victim for your anger. Plan for your anger and live in solution.

Andrea, Seth, Doris, Andrew

What could these four people have done differently to manage their emotional situation and keep their anger under control?

Seth completely disregarded the plans he made with Andrea for Friday night. He never thought to make a quick phone call to tell her he couldn't be home at 5:00 for their planned night of togetherness. Instead, Seth totally disregarded Andrea's feelings and went on about his way as if he has no responsibility to Andrea at all. Breaking plans with someone is acceptable; disregarding their feelings is never acceptable. You will never get a good response when you intentionally hurt others or disregard their feelings.

Andrea's anger was escalating the whole time she was unable to reach Seth. Mix in some worry and hurt feelings and you are bound to get strong emotions. Instead of hurling the phone at Seth, Andrea might have explained how she felt and how important that night was to her. She might have explained how Seth hurt her feelings by not showing up as planned and for not bothering to pick up the phone to call her. Anger is acceptable; aggression is never an acceptable form of expression.

Let's face it. Others can be just plain oblivious to your feelings. They get caught up in their own thoughts and feelings and forget about yours. There is no way for anyone to know how you are feeling unless you communicate your feelings in an assertive manner. Throwing the phone communicates something, but not what Andrea really wanted to say to Seth. The reaction you get from others when you communicate your feelings appropriately will be much different than if you act out your feelings in anger.

After journaling about her anger, Doris knows that her anger is really hurt and disappointment. Instead of dwelling on it, she calls a friend and her night goes on in solution. It might not be the most perfect night she was hoping for, but it certainly beats staying home and feeling angry.

Andrew is an impatient person. He knows his anger escalates out of control when he is put in a situation of waiting. Since Andrew already knows this about himself, how can he live in solution and plan his appointments differently to help keep his anger under control? He might plan to go to the doctor at less busy times. Making an appointment during lunch like everyone else tries to do is probably not a good idea for Andrew. He might try to call ahead to see if the doctor is running on time or how many people are in line in front of him. Maybe he could reschedule the appointment to be the first patient in the morning so he isn't waiting for others to be seen ahead of him. Good anger management is all about getting to know yourself very well and then finding ways to make you successful in life and living in solutions rather than living in the problem.

Be A People Watcher

If you are having problems seeing and rating your own anger, it might be easier to observe how others handle their anger. I am sure you have seen someone other than yourself in an angry state. You could turn on your television and see plenty of angry behavior in the comforts of your own home. Turn the volume down on the TV and just watch the body language and try to understand what anger really "looks" like.

What did they look like? How did they express their anger?

Did you see any behaviors similar to what you do when you are angry?

How would you rate their anger? Mild? Moderate? Strong?

It's Not All On The Inside

Not only do you experience internal signs or uncomfortable feelings when you are angry, there are also physical (outward) signs you need to become familiar with to help you manage your behavior. It can be very difficult to notice the internal, more subtle signs of anger in the beginning phases of anger management if you are not tuning into your emotions. If you cannot catch the internal signs yet; you will in time with dedication and practice. In the meantime, while you are practicing catching your inner emotions, watch for outward physical signs of your anger.

What are some outward signs of your anger? How do you display your anger? Think about how you feel inside when you are angry and then think about how you act out on your anger. What displays of your emotions have others noticed? Has anyone ever told you "you look really mad?" "Or, why are you so quiet?" What about the other people you observed when they were angry? What were their physical signs of anger?

Examples of physical signs of anger might be:

- Red face, feel hot, sweating.
- Tight jaws
- Arms crossed tightly in front.
- Racing pulse.
- Top of your head feels like it is pounding off.
- Chest pain.

40

- Silence (ignoring those talking to you and your surroundings).
- Throwing things.
- Slamming doors or objects.

Take a moment now and write in your journal or below how you feel emotionally and physically when you are angry. What have others told you look like when you are angry?

How I feel inside when I am angry:

_____

_____

_____

My physical signs of anger are:

_____

_____

_____

Others have told me I look:

_____

_____

_____

Examples could be:

"Your face is beat red!"
"Why are you grinding your jaws?"
"You seem so quiet today."
I feel like I am going to burst open.
My hands begin to shake.
I feel like running.
I get an instant headache.

Reading The Signs

The first step in learning to recognize different levels of anger is to become aware of your anger signs or anger triggers. The better you are at reading the signs and triggers the better you will become at rating and managing your anger. The more you practice and become aware of your emotions the more you will be able to recognize your anger automatically.

Not only is it critical to recognize your anger signs, but just as important to recognize when others are having problems in controlling their anger. Recognizing when others have problems with anger will help you withdraw from dangerous situations and avoid escalating confrontations. The last thing you want to do is get into a debate with an angry person who is having problems keeping their anger under their own control.

Once you have identified some of your triggers you will be able to work more constructively to control your response to those triggers. Anger triggering thoughts occur automatically so it will take some conscious work on your part to identify them.

People stop thinking clearly when they are angry and tend to make up their minds about a situation right away. Next they spend a great deal of energy and time focusing on how they feel and how the situation affects them. Instead of repeatedly paying attention your anger triggers keep yourself focused on understanding the situation you are faced with. You do not need to respond to every anger provoking situation right away. I refer to anger provoking situations as anger invitations. We are constantly being invited to become angry every day. The slow driver. The smart aleck who dismisses your concerns. The rude counter person. Don't accept every anger invitation. Instead, start to recognize the situation as an anger invitation. Step back, think and approach the situation in a prepared and relaxed manner. The more you deflect someone else's bad mood or anger, the more in control of the situation you become. There is strength in control.

Assignment For The Week

Take a full week to practice this chapter. There are no quick fixes; you must recognize the old behaviors to learn the new anger management techniques.

Keep writing in your journal. Become aware of your angry behavior and rate the intensity (mild, moderate, strong).

Review the entries in your journal on a daily basis and notice patterns and strengths of your anger.

Think of alternatives that can help you avoid situations that cause your anger to become strong and out of control. *LIVE IN SOLUTION*.

Think about the following questions:

How can you plan to avoid the things that anger you?

What triggers your anger?

What are your physical signs of anger?

Are you able to read your anger cues/signs?

Do you see any patterns in your anger?

42

Remember to look for your positive progress. Congratulate yourself when you do something well. Recognize your achievements. This is a tough process, but you are here and you are doing it.

What good things happened to you during the week? What did you like about your week/day? What worked for you today? What do you like about your life? What do you like about yourself?

Key Point: Stop justifying your anger and trying to make yourself "right." Justifying your anger takes a great deal of time and energy when you could be putting the effort into changing your life. Acting on each angry thought expends a great deal of energy and is destructive to your health and your most important relationships with others.

Key Point: Once you have identified some of your triggers and have begun to understand your trigger themes, you will be able to work more constructively to control your responses to those triggers.

Key Point: Anger triggering thoughts occur automatically and almost instantaneously so it will take conscious work to identify them and substitute new healthy thoughts and behaviors.

Key Point: If you encounter an anger trigger and your strategies for handling that trigger successfully didn't work, make a note of it. Think about what you would do differently the next time. If something you did worked for your anger trigger, include it into your anger plan.

Chapter 3

Warning! Warning!

- Rating your anger will alert you to situations that cause strong anger.
- There are internal and outward physical signs of anger.
- Words to describe mild or weak anger could be annoyed, irritated, frustrated.
- Words to describe moderate anger could be mad, pissed off, angry.
- Words to describe strong anger could be furious, boiling, enraged.
- Angry behavior does not always mean outward expressions or actions.
- Silence or "the silent treatment" could be a display of anger.
- We need anger in dangerous situations for survival.
- Anger can produce powerful positive changes.

I Saw The Sign…

There is just no way that we can be oblivious to warning signs in our modern world. We get warning signs everywhere we go and there are warning signs with almost every thing we own. If it plugs in or moves, you probably had to pay attention to or fix an annoying warning light. Just about everything you come in contact with today seems to come complete with a warning sign. Even we have warning signs if we are paying attention and catching ourselves in the act.

Some of the most popular warning lights that you meet up with on a daily basis are: on the dashboard of your car, railroad crossings, pedestrian crosswalks, computers, stop signs, walk, don't walk, school zones… Can you even imagine a world without signs? How would we know what to do?

Although you learned to recognize the warning signs mentioned above early on in your life, you probably never learned to recognize your own anger warning signs. Being aware and practicing while you are learning anger management will help you notice that you too have warning signs that can help you manage your anger before it gets out of control.

Doing Their Job

What is the first thing you usually do when you notice a warning sign on a piece of equipment is flashing? First of all, you probably sit up and take notice. It gets your attention. Secondly, you put some thought into what the problem could be and maybe even come up with options to fix it. Finally, you set out on a mission to fix the problem and restore the equipment to full working condition.

The most important job of the warning is that it makes you take notice.

Your Signs

Warning signs are what you first start to feel when you begin to experience stress and anger. While your warning signs may not be as obvious as flashing lights in the beginning of this process, with time and practice you will be able to rely on your warning signals and check out your emotions long before they escalate into more than just a warning.

The problem with warning signs is that most of us aren't sure of what they are. We don't pay attention to them or may not even recognize them until anger escalates out of control. By then the warning is definitely more than a warning and you have probably acted out without paying attention.

Can you think of some warning signs you may feel when you first start to get angry?

Examples: rapid heart beat, tense muscles, repeated negative thoughts, tight throat, neck pain, headaches, muscle tension, hot and flushed, temples pounding, rapid shallow breathing, sweaty palms...

Warning signs I notice when I am angry are:

_____

_____

Anger... It Does A Body Harm

Not only are you affected emotionally every time you experience anger, your body also experiences dramatic changes which chemically prepares you to run or fight. The basic mechanism of anger is a very primitive "fight or flight" response needed for human survival. When there is a perceived threat of bodily harm, the calm body switches over in response to fear, making us ready to fight. You might say your body has an automatic defense mechanism that can make you physically equipped to handle danger.

What Happens To Your Body

Like other emotions, anger is experienced in our bodies as well as our minds. There is a complex series of physiological events that occurs as you become angry.

When your fight or flight response gets activated, chemicals are released into your bloodstream. These chemicals cause your body to undergo very powerful changes. Breathing increases. Blood is detoured away from the organs you don't use in a fight and is directed into muscles that require extra energy for running and fighting. Pupils dilate to sharpen vision, awareness intensifies and your pain perception decreases.

You are now in your attack mode, emotionally or physically ready to run or fight. Your rational mind is disengaged and your thoughts are distorted, only thinking of survival.

When you are faced with real dangers in the world, this fight or flight response is invaluable to your survival. This chemical response was probably very much appreciated by our caveman ancestors when an intruder entered the cave. It was a necessary tool for survival to shoo away the unwanted predator and to prepare to run or fight.

Unfortunately, we have the same strong responses today as the caveman years ago, but in our modern world we are not usually faced with stampeding antelope. Although our modern day stressors may *feel* like real danger, they really don't require a strong physical reaction. The changes we are experiencing during "fight or flight" are gearing us up for battle when most times there really is no battle to fight.

This fight or flight preparation phase also has a wind down period. We eventually start to relax back towards our resting state when we may feel justified in committing an angry aggressive action. As you know, it may feel more satisfying to feel angry than to acknowledge the painful feelings associated with being vulnerable. Anger cannot make pain disappear, but it can cause serious health issues.

Anger Over And Over

Anger has a negative impact on your physical well-being. Chronically angry, hostile and irritable people are described as Type A personalities. People with more laid back personalities are usually described as Type B personality. Type A personalities are more likely to display aggressive and competitive personality traits. Type A personalities are more likely to develop serious heart disease, weakened immune systems and non repairable damage to the body's organs and tissues.

Type A Traits:

- Always in a hurry.
- Have little patience for other people.
- Unable to give their full attention to others.
- Tend to be critical and judgmental.
- Focuses on the weaknesses of others.
- Unable to tolerate incompetence of others.

Some of you are probably thinking to yourself that your Type A personality makes you driven and has helped you succeed to become the person you are today. That would probably be true, but you need to acquire a healthy balance. Being in a constant state of high energy or experiencing chronic anger will eventually take its toll on you physically.

Chronic anger equals constant anger. In other words, you never get over feeling angry. Constant anger takes a toll your body in that the chemicals your body releases for the fight or flight response accumulate and make your body pay a price for being in a constant high energy state for extended periods of time. The long-term physical affects of chronic anger could involve:

- People with chronic anger are more likely to have suppressed immune systems. Properly functioning immune systems are needed to keep you healthy and disease free.
- Since many chronically angry people also suffer from chronic stress, they are more at risk for gastrointestinal problems such as irritable bowel syndrome and ulcers.
- Chronic anger can also lead to cardiovascular disease and heart disease such as heart attacks and stroke.
- Anger can affect your blood pressure and over time can lead to kidney problems.
- By recognizing the signs and symptoms of being in fight or flight, you can take the steps to manage the overload.

Try to think of a time when you felt angry recently. Look in your journal and think of the following: what did you physically feel like while angry, how did your body respond and how you may have appeared to others while angry. Maybe someone even had the courage to tell you what you looked like.

It is important that you recognize the difference in your physical body when you are calm as opposed to when you are angry.

Examples of physical signs of anger you might have experienced are:

Tense muscles, tight throat, rapid heartbeat, neck pain, headaches, throbbing and pounding in your temples, feeling hot, fast breathing.

What are your physical signs of anger?

_____
_____
_____

Think about what you were doing to trigger your anger.

I was _____ when I started to feel angry. My physical signs of anger were:

_____
_____
_____

Example:

I was standing in the grocery check out line when I first started to feel angry. The clerk was extremely slow and the customer ahead of me did not have enough money to pay her bill and was slowly searching through her purse. I was in a hurry because I had an appointment and I was already running late.

Physical Signs

Arms crossed in front of me, sweaty palms, making fists, standing on one leg and then the other, restless legs, foot tapping and pacing side to side, tight neck and shoulders, facial tension, rolling eyes, face hot and flushed.

Stress Reduction Techniques

Stress takes a serious toll on your body and if it is left uncontrolled will either destroy you physically or socially when you eventually act out your anger. Over time stress can create depression, anxiety, pessimism, and dissatisfaction. It can also make you difficult to live with because people under stress are usually irritable, irrational and hostile.

Change of any kind can induce stress because of: fear of the unknown, insecurity, fear of rejection, the need for approval, fear of conflict, fear of developing trust, and fear of inability to cope with change just to name a few. There are also individual personality characteristics that can induce stress which include: low self esteem, loss of control, fear of being judged, chronic striving to be perfect, chronic guilt, chronic anger and depression.

Stress can also be caused by a multitude of things such as lack of an adequate support system, lack of healthy communication in your relationships, struggle for power or control, chronic conflict and disagreements with no healthy resolution. I am sure you are thinking of a few things in your own life that have caused you stress over the years. The physical signs of stress are very much the same as the fight or flight mechanism you experience when you are angry. Because of the physical and emotion toll stress takes it is imperative that you implement your relaxation techniques on a daily basis.

It is also very helpful to be active in your day. Exercise helps to eliminate stress hormones from the bloodstream and stimulates the release of endorphins which provide a feeling of well-being. Avoid stimulants. Stimulants such as caffeine, nicotine, and alcohol stress out the body and can make you more irritable and impatient. Instead, drink a lot of water and try herbal teas. Make time to laugh. Find humor in your life and implement fun activities. Tell a joke and laugh at yourself from time to time.

Time Management

Why are we talking about so many different issues in this book when it is really an anger management plan we are trying to achieve? There are so many issues in your day that can contribute to your anger or stress level. Since we are making a plan for your life we need to mention and be thinking of everything that can bring on stress and anger triggers.

When you do not use your time efficiently and you are constantly on the treadmill of going here and going there without little regard for your emotions or physical well-being you are inviting stress and anger into your life. So many people spend their days in a frenzy of activity, but achieve very little because they're not concentrating their effort on the things that matter the most.

Time management is an endless series of decisions that shape your day. Inappropriate decisions produce frustration, low self-esteem, and increased stress. Symptoms of poor time management include: procrastination, fatigue, rushing from one place to the other without really accomplishing anything, insufficient personal time or relaxation, and doing what you *have* to do instead of what you want to do.

In your journal, take a time inventory. I would like for you to write down your priorities for the day. Establish priorities that highlight your most important goals for the day. Base your decisions on what is important to you and what is not important to your day. Be realistic about your achievements and prioritize your tasks. Begin by eliminating low priority issues.

Start to make time for yourself and learn to say *no.* Stay away from low priority commitments. Get up an hour earlier and plan your day. Have quiet time to yourself before the rush of your day begins and make a conscious effort not to procrastinate. Learn to make decisions for yourself and get active in carrying out your tasks.

Many people have told me that they have difficulty in making decisions for themselves because they were made to feel blamed or criticized for the choices they made in childhood. They leave the decision making to others and do not go out on the limb and make choices for themselves. The real problem here is other people don't know exactly what you need and want in your life. Even though you may have felt helpless to make decisions as a child you are not a helpless adult. Don't procrastinate on the decisions in your life. Take responsibility for your life and decide for yourself which direction you need to take to be a successful adult in your day.

I say so many times to parents who have children with discipline problems to add structure into their homes. Children sometimes experience behavioral difficulties when they do not experience stability and structure in the home. They act out because they feel stressed and frightened as to "what's going to happen next?" I start by asking parents to implement a set structure so that children know what to expect in their day. Routine brings comfort to children and over the years I have come to find that structure, routine and time management have profound and positive influences on adults as well. Remember that anger management is about planning. Don't set yourself up for stress and anger triggers by running endlessly in your day. Plan your days, learn to prioritize, realize that you are not Superman or Wonder Woman and learn to say no to low priority activities.

Time management is really more than just managing your time; it is managing ourselves in relation to time. It is about setting priorities and taking charge of your situation and time utilization. It means changing those habits or activities that cause us to waste time. It is about being willing to experiment with different methods and ideas to enable you to find the best way to make maximum the use of your time.

Recognizing Your Behavior

Recognizing your own behavior is one of the most important processes in learning to manage your anger. Remember in Chapter One, when you were challenged to think of some things you may need to change in order to make your life a happier place to be? Some of you may already know what you needed to change in your life before entering this program. Some of you will be gathering this information along the way by paying close attention to your behavior and emotions in the process. Gathering information and learning about your emotions requires your personal commitment. A commitment to changing your life and becoming proactive in the process means you are willing to take notice of your emotions that have been on automatic pilot for a very long time. A commitment to changing your live also means you are willing and ready to replace old behaviors with healthy new behaviors and rational thoughts.

In addition to physical costs of anger we spoke about earlier there are also significant social and emotional costs to being angry all of the time. Hostile, angry people are less likely to experience healthy supportive relationships than are less hostile people. Angry people have fewer friends, are more likely to become depressed, and are more likely to become verbally or physically abusive toward others. Chronically angry people do not experience intimacy in their personal relationships and their partners and family members tend to be more guarded and less able to relax around them. Angry people also have cynical attitudes toward others are unable to recognize or utilize support when it is available.

One of the biggest costs of anger is that angry people do not realize that their behavior is pushing people away and therefore fill the void with drinking, using drugs, smoking and eating more than those who have fulfilling relationships.

Accepting Personal Responsibility

When you hear the word responsibility what do you first think of? Who's responsible for this? Who did it? Let's shift that thinking over to redefining responsibility as seizing opportunity, having choices and taking control of your life. Responsibility is about going out and creating what you want through personal choices.

We are one hundred percent responsible for how our lives turn out. When things are going well we are more than happy to take the responsibility for our successes. When things aren't going so well we are just as quick to point the finger to blame someone else for our short comings. The responsibility for your life is in your own hands and serious change requires serious courage.

Because you have freedom of choice and because you have chosen each and every circumstance in your adult life, you are completely responsible for all of your success and failures, your happiness and unhappiness, your present and your future.

The opposite of accepting responsibility is making excuses. Placing blame on people and things for what's going on in your own life. When you remain irresponsible in life you are subjecting yourself to becoming angry, hostile, fearful, resentful and stuck in unhappiness. When you accept responsibility for growth and change your mind calms, you see things differently, your emotions calm and you are able to think more positively and constructively. You gain insight into your life!

What Is Accepting Responsibility?

- Acknowledging that you are solely responsible for the choices in your life.
- Accepting that you are responsible for what you choose to feel or think.
- Accepting that you cannot blame others for the choices you make.
- Realizing that you determine your feelings about events and people.
- Letting go of blame and anger toward those in your past.
- Working out anger, hostility and pessimism over hurts, pain, and mistreatment.
- Accepting the belief that you are responsible for determining who you are, and how your choices affect your life.
- Taking the time for personal development and growth.

How Can Failing To Accept Personal Responsibility Result In Negative Consequence?

- You are angry, hostile and depressed over how unfairly you have been treated.
- You remain fearful of change or decision making.
- You become overwhelmed by disabling fears and thoughts.
- You become emotionally and physically unhealthy.
- You may begin to rely on alcohol, drugs, food, gambling, sex, and smoking.
- You may feel unable to trust others or feel secure.

What Behaviors Need To Be Developed In Order To Accept Personal Responsibility?

- Find and accept help for yourself.
- Be open to new ideas and implementing change in your life.
- Give yourself positive feedback.
- Let go of anger, fear, blame, mistrust and negative self talk.
- Reorganize your priorities and goals.
- Realize that you are in charge of the direction your life takes.

Once you know what you want and commit yourself to personal achievement, you are able to avoid all discomfort due to resistance to change. You will develop new habits and know that things just "do not just" happen without you. You are the one who makes your life happen. Taking personal responsibility is not an option.

Assignment For The Week

Continue writing in your journal.

Notice your warning signs, internal signs and physical signs of anger. The very next time you have a warning, stop and think of your options. Make an effort to do something about the warnings before they get out of your control.

Write about your anger options in your journal and decide if they worked for you. If they didn't work, think of other options that may have worked better or how you might handle situations in the future. If they did work, pat yourself on the back for living in solution.

Challenge yourself to pay attention to your behavior every day.

Think about the following questions:

What are your early signs of anger?

What happens to your body when you experience anger?

Can you recognize your own behaviors?

What good things happened to you during the week? What did you like about your week/day? What worked for you today? What do you like about your life? What do you like about yourself?

Key Point: Our brains are wired in such a way to influence us to act before we can properly consider the consequences of our actions. This is not an excuse for behaving badly. People can and do control their aggressive impulses and you can to with awareness and practice. Managing anger has to be learned. We are not born angry and most of us are not taught how to manage our anger. Managing your anger is not instinctual, it is an acquired skill.

Key Point: Taking personal responsibility is not an option.

Key Point: Stress takes a serious toll on your body and if it is left uncontrolled will either destroy you physically or you will eventually act out your anger and it will destroy you socially. Over time stress can create depression, anxiety, pessimism, and dissatisfaction. It can also make you difficult to live with because people under stress are irritable, irrational and hostile.

Key Point: Chronic anger equals constant anger. In other words, you never get over feeling angry. Constant anger takes a toll your body in that the chemicals your body releases for the fight or flight response accumulate and make your body pay a price for being in a constant high energy state for extended periods of time.

Key Point: Warning signs are what you first start to feel when you begin to experience stress and anger. While your warning signs may not be as obvious as flashing lights in the beginning of this process, with time and practice you will be able to rely on your warning signals and check out your emotions long before they escalate into more than just a warning.

Chapter 4

Is It Really Anger?

- Physical signs of anger are a warning to pay close attention to your behavior.
- Your physical displays of anger are noticed by those around you.
- Learning to recognize your own behavior is a very important process in managing your anger.
- Anger can take a serious toll on your physical well-being.
- Chronic anger can lead to heart disease and strokes.
- Your body has a survival mechanism called "fight or flight" to help engage you in battle.
- Strong chemical reactions in your body occur each time you experience anger.
- Recognizing your anger signs will help you to plan better outcomes.

Focus

Experiencing and expressing emotions are an important part of your life. Properly identifying the exact emotion can be difficult for most people and even more difficult to express appropriately.

When you experience an emotion (good or bad), your thoughts, perceptions and senses all quickly guide you to respond in certain protective ways. The actual emotional and physical reaction that you display may be more related to the *interpretation* of events rather than to the actual event itself.

For example, if you are guided into a dark room and suddenly the lights came on and people jumped out at you, you may first interpret the situation as one that you need to defend yourself and start swinging. You would probably feel *fear* of being in an unknown circumstance or surroundings. When a group of your friends sing the happy birthday song and you get to unwrap presents you would quickly realize that you are no longer in danger and you would shift your thoughts from fear to happy surprise.

Identifying accurately what is happening around you requires you to quickly focus on the situation. You will need to focus on exactly what you are feeling rather than acting out behaviors immediately and without thought. If you do not take that one second to identify the feeling, your responses (physically and emotionally) can become exaggerated and quickly out of your control. Many people slip into acting out their behaviors because they do not take a second to think, evaluate the situation and engage their rational brain.

Identifying the exact emotion correctly will require you to engage your brain and quickly focus closely on yourself and your feelings in the event. As an example, a teenager taking anger management told me recently that the reason he was taking anger management was because he was playing football and right when he was about to throw the ball his buddy came up behind him and pushed him to the ground. The teenager picked himself up and started swinging at his buddy as the perceived threat. I asked him, "Were you angry in that moment?" He replied, "No, anger never even entered my mind. I was scared and now I have to take anger management!" How would things have been different for him if he would have taken a second before reacting? We often perceive emotions in the moment without thinking about our reactions. The goal here is to take one second to engage your rational brain to help determine exactly what you are feeling and experiencing so that you can express yourself appropriately. Match your behavior to the situation.

What Else Could It Be?

Is it really anger or could it be something else? Other emotions that can bring about the same responses as anger are: fear, and surprise. Whether you are experiencing fear, anger or surprise, your body can automatically respond with the same powerful response (fight or flight) for each of these emotions.

Remember in Chapter Three when we discussed "fight or flight" as the response your body is gearing up for battle and the many changes you feel? There is a strong relationship in how your body reacts to fear, anger and surprise. While they are all very different emotions, your body can automatically respond the same to all three if you are not paying attention.

You need to be the judge of your surroundings and quickly bring the situation under your own control to decide which emotion you are feeling and act accordingly. The physical signs of fear, surprise and anger are similar, but the outcomes as you can imagine are very different. Let's take a look.

Fear... the other emotion

Fear: an unpleasant often strong emotion caused by anticipation or awareness of danger.

When a person confronts real danger, fear can be an important means of self-preservation. The fight or flight mechanism kicks in and equips your body with incredible strength and ability to get away from danger.

Tale Of The Fearful Caveman

Imagine a caveman sitting near a small fire in the comfort of his cave. Suddenly, he sees the shadow of a lion in the light of his fire. His body reacts instantly. To survive, the caveman has to make a decision to either fight or run. The automatic response of fight or flight kicks in for the caveman to prepare him for battle.

A quick review of the fight or flight response we learned in the previous Chapter:

- Digestion slows so that blood can be directed to the muscles and the brain. It is more important to be alert and strong in the face of danger than to digest food. Have you ever felt butterflies in your stomach?
- Breathing gets faster to supply more oxygen for the needed muscles. Can you remember a time when you could not catch your breath after being frightened?
- The heart speeds up, and blood pressure soars, forcing blood to parts of the body that need it. Have you ever felt your heart pounding?
- Perspiration increases to cool the body. This allows the body to burn more energy.
- Muscles tense in preparation for important action. Have you ever had a stiff neck after a stressful day?
- Chemicals are released to make the blood clot more rapidly. If one is injured, this clotting can reduce blood loss.
- Sugars and fats pour into the blood to provide fuel for quick energy. Have you ever been surprised by your strength and endurance during an emergency?

For the caveman living in a cave and facing many environmental stressors, this fight or flight response was very valuable for survival. Today, we are seldom faced with the same type of danger the caveman experienced, but we still have the same and just as powerful fight or flight response as the caveman.

Take a moment now and think about a time when you experienced fear. Think about what you felt like physically and emotionally. Did you act out with anger? Did you feel any physical symptoms of fight or flight? (Racing heart beat, rapid breathing etc.)

I felt fear because of _____ and I acted out physically and emotionally by

_____

_____

Personal Fear Example

I hate to fly! On a flight west several years ago, I experienced a patch of extremely rough turbulence which lasted for several hours and I was miserable. The fact that I hate to fly doesn't stop me from traveling because I need to get to various destinations frequently, but it still doesn't change the fact that I experience fear when I fly.

In order to make flying tolerable for me, I have to focus on the best way to handle my fear in flight. Through experience and self study, I found that remaining quiet, thinking positive thoughts, deep breathing (relaxation techniques) and reading can make flying tolerable for me. I made an exact science out of living in a solution and focusing on finding ways to make the experience as pleasant as I possibly can even though I still don't like to fly.

Realizing discomfort I experience is more due to fear than any other emotion, I begin living in solution and practicing positive self-talk… repeating the mantra that I am safe, this is one of the safest forms of transportation… taking deep breaths, diverting my attention to reading. I can get through the flight fairly well if I am focusing on and understanding my emotions.

While I am going through my positive self talk ritual, I know the following: I am emotionally unavailable to engage in small talk with others, that I need to concentrate on my emotions and solutions to keep my fear under control, that I need a "time out" from external stimulation so that I can concentrate and not act out my fear. I also know from past experiences that engaging with others when I have fear actually makes the fear stronger. I have spent the time and energy getting the basic information I need to make myself successful in these types of situations.

On my last flight, as luck would have it, the flight was extremely turbulent. As we began tossing around from the turbulence, I automatically started my positive self-talk. I started to live in solution. While I am involved in my living in solution, wouldn't you know the lady sitting right next to me who didn't speak for the whole trip decides that she needs to talk during this time? My time out period! She started off with, "Isn't this great! I love to fly! Have you ever had so much fun?" "I remember a time… She never stopped talking about how great the turbulence was and how much she enjoyed getting tossed around in the sky until we landed.

What do you think that did to my fear level? Although I tried to be aware of my emotions and my reactions to those emotions, my fear took one step further into mild anger. I tried to nonchalantly let the passenger know several times I was not available to chat with her during this stressful time, but she never took the hint. I eventually had to slightly turn my back to her so that I could ignore her and think about how much I hated a woman that I didn't even know for doing this to me. How dare she talk to me when I am feeling this stressed out?

Rational Thinking

Did I really hate this woman? Of course not! Did she cause my anger? No. Was I feeling anger? No it was not anger that I was it experiencing. I was feeling fear and she for sure wasn't responsible for my fear. Did she know that I was trying to self-talk myself down to safety? No. Was it her responsibility to guess that I was having a problem? No.

Should she have realized that I was angry? If she was good at reading warning signs of anger she might have realized I was having a problem, but who really understands another person's reactions unless there is communication. Once I realized my level of fear was escalating I had a responsibility to communicate my problem assertively so that I could gain her understanding rather than turn my back in anger and internalize my thoughts and fears.

After we finally landed, I attempted to explain to the other passenger that I have a tremendous fear of flying and that I was unavailable to carry on a conversation with her at the moment she wanted to talk. As you can guess, she wasn't very interested in carrying on a conversation with me anymore either. Fear can quickly slip into irrational thoughts and anger if you are not sure how to deal with it. It takes practice and hard work, but we are all very capable of doing it. As Maya Angelou so eloquently puts it, "You did then what you knew how to do and when you knew better... you did better!" I'll do better the next time

Now it's your turn to think of a time when you had fear that turned into angry behavior.

I felt fear because of _____ and I acted:

_____
_____
_____
_____

Surprise, Surprise, Surprise

Surprise: to attack unexpectedly, an unexpected attack, to cause astonishment.

Surprise is another emotion that everyone has had the luxury of experiencing.

While the definition of surprise uses "unexpected attack", surprise isn't really a physical threat or attack to us at all. However, when you experience surprise, your body can quickly react with the same automatic and powerful reaction, fight or flight as with fear and anger. As you are becoming aware of your emotions and you are paying close attention in this behavioral change process, you may find yourself acting out in ways that are inappropriate to the actual event you are experiencing.

When you find yourself in these intense situations, quickly ask yourself:

1. Am I in danger? If so, remove yourself from the situation immediately.
2. What emotion am I really feeling?
3. What does my body feel like right now?
4. Are my feelings exaggerated for the situation?
5. Am I acting out inappropriately to the actual event?

3 Steps to help you quickly interpret your emotions:

- Evaluate the event.
- Interpret the event correctly.
- Respond appropriately.

Can you see the similarities in the physical reactions and emotions of fear, anger and surprise? It is very important to quickly judge the emotion you are experiencing to keep you from acting out in stressful situations and taking your emotions one step further into anger. This is tough work and it takes time, practice, desire and energy to put this much thought into your behavior. It is also very necessary work in understanding yourself and your emotions.

Another Example

I have a friend who warned anyone who might have the courage to throw her a surprise birthday party that it would never be appreciated or welcomed. However, because she is such a lovely person, a group of people decided to ignore her warnings and gave her a beautifully catered birthday bash with all the trimmings. One friend took her shopping while all the guests arrived. When she got home and walked into her dark surroundings, she had no idea there were hiding guests ready to jump out and surprise her with their presence.

When the lights suddenly came on and all the screaming started, my friend within one second, started swinging her fists and wildly kicking the friend who took her shopping. She kicked and kicked her until someone ran up and pulled her away. Without thought, she quickly interpreted the surprise situation as a dangerous (fear) situation and started beating her friend.

Remember that physically we feel an automatic response to fear, anger and surprise. It is for that one brief moment that we need to stop and evaluate if we are in danger and have fear or are we just shocked and surprised. Given some time and practice you will become good in judging the difference between fear and surprise and anger or any other emotions you experience in the moment.

Take a moment now and think of a time when someone or something surprised you and made you have fear for a brief moment until you were able to distinguish what was really going on.

I was surprised by _____ and felt

_____

_____

_____

One of my favorite examples: A father taking anger management told me recently that he always seemed to shout at his children and didn't know why. He didn't mean to shout at the kids, but his wife told him that he better get his "anger" under control or risk not spending time with his kids at all. When he came to the program, I asked him about his feelings and why he felt he was angry especially around his children. He was perplexed because he said he never felt "anger" around his children at all, but he did notice that he seemed to yell and scream a lot which in turn frightened his children. After recapping and delving deeper into his feelings, Michael realized that he was having the most problem with his emotions at times when his kids would do things to put them in danger or would hurt themselves. When his kids fell off of the monkey bars at the park, he would yell and scream… not because he was angry, because he felt fear. He felt fear which caused him to act out his emotions by yelling and screaming. Yelling was his immediate reaction to the fear he felt. However, when he yelled and screamed at the kids out of fear of hurting themselves; everyone perceived Michael as an angry individual with a severe anger problem. Michael, in time, was able to recognize his fear as a strong emotion and was able to quickly recognize when he felt fear and devised techniques to live in solution rather than yell and scream. It wasn't easy for Michael to change a behavior he used for a very long time, but he wanted to make positive changes in his life for himself and his children so that they all could live in solution. Michael continues to monitor his behavior on a daily basis and works on improving his relationship with his children. He is living in solution and is a work in progress!

Read the examples below and try to determine which emotion the people may be experiencing (fear, anger or surprise):

Andrew

Andrew is always late getting to work. His boss told him that if he is late one more time, he would risk getting suspended. Andrew liked his job and didn't want to be suspended, but he also had a problem getting up in the morning and getting to work on time. Because he was late again, Andrew was driving at a high rate of speed to beat the clock.

Out of nowhere, a car came out of a cross street causing Andrew to slam on his brakes sliding wildly out of control. He barely missed the car. He sat there for a moment dazed and confused. All of a sudden Andrew bolted out of the car and began kicking the other persons car frantically, screaming obscenities at the top of his lungs at the other driver.

60

Andrew probably felt (fear, anger or surprise)?

_____

Janice

Janice loved to shop. She loved to shop from the time she got up in the morning to late at night. I guess you could say it was her passion. One day, Janice was in her favorite store looking through racks of clothing when all of a sudden the rack she was looking at started to wobble and suddenly collapsed to the floor with a thud barely missing her foot. Janice jumped back several feet staring at all the bargains lying on the floor. Without any thought Janice began kicking at the rack on the floor and calling it all sorts of names. A clerk noticed that Janice was having a problem and came over to see if she could help. Janice abruptly told her that she was stupid for putting a rack in the store that was broken and that the rack could have killed her.

Janice probably felt (fear, anger or surprise)?

_____

Grover

Grover planned a business meeting a month in advance. He asked all of the participants to clear their schedules so that they would be available to attend. No one reported back to Grover that the date conflicted with their schedule. This meeting was very important to the company as they were meeting new clients for the very first time. The employees were to provide a presentation to help sell the company.

None of the employees showed up to the meeting and Grover was left to conduct the meeting by himself. Grover could feel his heart pounding, sweaty palms, and tension in all of his muscles. On Monday morning, Grover met with his employees to find out why no one bothered to show up for the meeting. One at a time the employees all told Grover that they had other commitments and were unable to attend. Grover screamed at them and told them that they were all a bunch of dumb idiots and that he hated them all.

Grover probably felt (fear, anger or surprise)?

_____

EXAMPLE BETWEEN FEAR, SURPRISE AND ANGER

Is it one emotion or all three emotions at work in the following example? As you read through the next example put yourself in the story and try to think of how you might have reacted or how you may have felt in this same situation.

A few days ago, I had the benefit of witnessing a first hand experience of fear, surprise and anger in a public parking lot. I was pulling into a parking space, looking down and not really paying close attention to where I was driving. Have you ever had your hand slip off the wheel and land on the horn at the worst of times? As I proceeded to pull into the parking space, I accidentally honked the horn strategically when a man was walking in front of my car. The man wasn't in any great danger because he was on the sidewalk and I was in the parking lot, but when I looked up he was bravely waving the middle finger wildly in the air at me and screaming words I wouldn't repeat.

For a moment I was stunned and taken back by his reaction. I sat there wondering what caused this guy to have such an angry response when it hit me that I scared him by accidentally honking the horn. The guy felt fear and he had an unsupervised fearful reaction.

The following might be his perception of what happened: he was leisurely walking along, probably having a nice day, having his own thoughts when I scared and surprised the heck out of him by accidentally honking the horn. The man instantly perceived that he was in danger and acted on it quickly by waving his club (the middle finger) just like a caveman might have years ago wildly in the air telling me to stay away.

Was the man really in any physical danger? "I" knew that he wasn't in any physical danger, but he quickly perceived that he was being physically assaulted and because he thought he was assaulted he acted out with angry behavior to protect himself.

Can you see how easy it is to confuse fear and surprise and why it can quickly develop into anger? Would it be fair to say that the man in the parking lot had fear and surprise that quickly turned into angry behavior?

Recap

Let's briefly recap the situation:

The man was walking on a sidewalk in public where people were shopping and eating. When I honked the horn, he jolted and made some kind of weird dance move I have not seen since the 70's and he looked foolish because he was scared. He felt fear and surprise.

Did I physically threaten him? No.

62

Did I surprise him? Yes. Did I scare him? Yes.

Even more so, did my actions embarrass him? Yes. Did I insult his emotional well being? Yes.

His anger forced him to do something back to me to help heal his pride. He took charge; he was going to get "me" now. That's how anger works if you don't stop to think about it. Anger can quickly escalate out of control without your constant attention.

Why

Why are we discussing emotions other than anger? Being aware of your behaviors and writing in your journal will help you to better understand that anger can be caused by many other emotions such as fear and surprise. Anger is a secondary emotion. You first have a thought and the thought leads to a feeling which can lead to a variety of acting out behaviors. The goal is to put a space between the feeling and the reaction. In that space lies your wisdom. The goal for your space is to engage your wisdom (brain) and understand exactly what you are feeling so that your reactions will match the situation.

Since it is the behavior you display that can quickly get you into trouble when you are experiencing a bad feeling; learning to become a good judge of what is happening around you will help you quickly gain control of your anger. Paying close attention to **all** of your emotions will help to keep your anger under your own control.

Remember Andrea from Chapter Two? She was angry with her husband Seth because he didn't come home when he promised. What other emotions could Andrea have experienced other than anger? If you said that Andrea's feelings were probably hurt, she felt let down, sad, fearful of Seth's well being... you have identified other emotions that may have caused her angry behavior. Remember: Thought... feeling...behavior.

When you are able to accurately decide what you are feeling, your reactions will be appropriate for that feeling. In Andrea's case, if she had realized that she was hurt, worried or sad; she may have been able to talk to Seth about her angry feelings instead of hurling the phone. Seth would probably have had a totally different reaction to Andrea's emotions and their night might have gone on as planned.

You Be The Judge

When you get warning signs, quickly determine if you are in physical danger. If you are in danger remove yourself from the situation immediately. If you are not in physical danger, try to not let your emotions escalate into uncontrolled angry behavior. Look for solutions while your feelings are mild and when you are able to think rationally.

Go back to your journal now and look at each entry. For each time you wrote that you experienced anger take a few seconds now to think of another emotion (fear, surprise, sadness etc.) you may have been feeling other than anger. Think of what you just learned in this chapter about fear, surprise and anger. Did you experience fear? Were you stressed out? Surprised? What exactly were you feeling? Identifying your feelings accurately and quickly will help you to control and manage your physical behavior.

Display Of Anger

In Chapter One of this book, you learned that anger is a normal, healthy emotion, but it is the behavior that you display when you are angry that can get you into trouble if you are not monitoring your reactions. Let's shift gears in this chapter and talk about what you may look like physically when you display angry behavior. While it is important that you are aware of your emotions, it is just as important to understand the types of behavior you display when you are angry.

Some people have told me that they have difficulty with this part of anger management because they do not "display" angry behavior. They don't throw things, hit people, scream or fly the middle finger. As you have learned, you do not need to have extreme and wild displays of anger to behave badly. Ignoring people, humming, avoiding eye contact, sulking, falsely agreeing with others are just a few non-violent ways to display anger. You will learn more about different anger types in upcoming chapters, but for now realize that acting out in anger takes many forms and they are not all physical.

If you put some thought into it and you are being honest with yourself, I bet you will come up with several types of behavior you display when you are angry. If you can't admit your behavior to others, start by admitting it to yourself. Admitting your behavior to yourself is the first step of behavioral change.

Ways that I display anger are:

_____

_____

_____

The First Sign

When you first begin to experience anger, your signs might be very mild and not easy to pick up on without your keen attention. Mild first signs of anger could be: humming, ignoring the person you are angry with, not talking to others around you, turning your back on someone, shutting people out.

Think of a time when you were irritated with someone and write down the behavior you displayed while you were miffed.

In your journal, you have been writing about your physical signs of anger. Now try to become aware of and write about the behavioral signs that you display when you are angry.

64

I was mildly angry with/at _____ so I

_____

_____

_____

I was moderately angry with/at _____ so I

_____

_____

_____

I felt strong anger with/at _____ so I

_____

_____

_____

Some questions to ask yourself to help you with this assignment:

- What were your early warning signs when you were first starting to get angry or irritated?
- Did you pay attention to your early warning lights?
- In looking back, can you recognize that you were getting angry by the behavior you displayed? (Some examples may be: turning your back and humming, trying to shut out the offender?)
- Would the situation have turned out differently for you or better for you if you recognized these early warning signs?
- Would you be able to stop yourself from letting your anger get out of control?
- If you could have known then what you know now, would you have been able to keep your anger manageable?

Recognition Is The Key In Managing Your Anger

Many people have told me that they do not experience early signs of anger; they just explode impulsively without warning signs or thoughts of anger. With what you already know and have learned in anger management this far, what would you tell them? Let me give you a hint: you might tell them if they were paying close attention to their emotions and thoughts they would realize that there **are** subtle signs of anger long before they actually explode in anger. Nothing is more important in learning to manage your own behavior than realizing when it is starting to get out of control even if it is only in your thoughts. If you can recognize it, you are capable of changing it.

Learn to trust your inner wisdom as you learn and grow in your life's changes. Trust and rely on what you are learning about yourself in this process and you will build your self esteem along the way. You know when you are having a bad thought and you know when you are about to act out in hurt or anger. When you learn to trust your inner guide, you are making the statement to yourself that you know what is best for you and you are in charge of your life. Learning to manage your anger means taking control of your life.

Other People

Many people try to place blame for their own anger on other people. Have you ever heard or experienced someone placing blame for their bad feelings? It is the "other" person's fault when they get angry and so "they" must be the ones with the anger problem and not them. I think the most popular blame I have heard throughout the years is that ex-spouses cause people to have huge difficulties in managing their anger. The truth is this…no one causes you to react or act out unless you are a willing participant. You engage with other people because you are willing to join their dance. You hold complete power and control over your own behaviors and no one else has the power to make you do anything you don't want to do. No one can make you do anything you are not willing to do when you are in control of your life and in control of your emotions.

If you feel as though other people are pushing you into reactions you don't want to be having, it is time to gain control of your behavior by finding solutions that work for you. Maybe a time out to get away from the heated situation would work for you? Maybe minimizing contact with a certain person will do the trick? Maybe you need to learn how to let issues go and move on in solution? You will need to determine what is right for you and your life circumstances, but don't live in problems when you are fully capable of finding solutions to make you a happier person. Just remember… if you are proactive in your life, you never rely on another person to make you happy and never give someone else the power to control your emotions. Get committed in this process and listen to yourself and rely on you to make yourself happy.

Understanding Others

As adults, we need to share a common goal of understanding our differences and work toward the acceptance of otherness. How can you begin the process of otherness? First of all, work toward accepting the fact that everyone has their own unique thought process. While other's thoughts and ideas may not match yours, no one is "wrong" or should be made to feel badly for having their own thoughts and feelings. Everyone feels good when they are honored for their thoughts and otherness. Secondly, no one can be absolutely correct all of the time and no one's ideas are superior to another person's thoughts. Everyone operates individually from past experiences and everyone lives in their own thought "comfort zone."

Comfort zones are developed uniquely by each of us as we learn and grow in our lives and our zones might not always be in sync with another person's beliefs. Remember, your thoughts aren't wrong, but you may need to work toward accepting that others think differently from you and live in their own comfort zone. Allowing others to be individuals and separate from your thought process will greatly help you to separate yourself and the need to be "right." Each time you disagree with someone or try to push your point only convinces the other person that **he** is correct and you are the one who isn't interpreting the situation correctly. This type of interaction engages you in battle for no reason and it breaks down relationships and intimacy.

The fact that we are each controlled by our own thought processes doesn't mean we have to mow others down or force them into our own beliefs. You don't have to see eye to eye with someone else all of the time. Once you accept the idea that no one else is going to interpret life exactly like you, you will spend less time attempting to change others and move into a more positive direction in your own life. You will never be successful in changing others who don't want to be changed, but you can be successful in changing yourself.

You will always experience insulting and critical people in the world at work, stores, freeways... who will not want to share your thoughts and opinions. You need to decide how big of a role you want them to play in your anger and in your life. Remember if they "make" *you* act out in an angry way, then it is *you* who paid the price. You control yourself and you are responsible for your behavior not them! Read this paragraph over and over until you understand that you are the responsible party for your own behavior and remember; rather than becoming annoyed because someone isn't like you, allow the differences and walk away.

Letting Go Of Your Thoughts

Our brain is continually working in an attempt to make sense out of our past, present and future. There may have been times when your childhood memories pop up and you spend time dwelling on the past. Maybe you take time to think about how bad your childhood was and how it still affects your adulthood today. Or, maybe you regret the way you were raised and think if you were brought up differently things would be better for you now as an adult. Many feel as though they had dysfunctional parents and rough childhood or harsh experiences which impede their chance for a happy adulthood. Of course everyone's childhood has an affect on them, but you can only use the excuse for so long. Becoming proactive in your life means that you begin to process the information and move forward in solutions that can make you a happier adult today. Contrary to what you might believe, personal happiness does not depend on life dealing you a good hand. How you respond to what comes your way will largely determine whether your life is fulfilling or not.

If you stay in your thoughts, you will stay in your past. If you become proactive in looking for ways to make yourself happier as an adult you will live in the present. Bad things do happen in childhood and life in general. However, right now, today in this moment, they are only your thoughts. Becoming a proactive inner directed person lies within your own thinking.

There may be times when thoughts of shame and guilt over past incidents or bad behaviors could consume you to the point of creating anger and low self esteem. I am often told in anger management sessions that people can't get beyond what brought them to anger management and the thoughts of self forgiveness are out of the question. We have a tendency to hold onto the bad because our inner critic tells us that our behavior is bad and we deserve to continue being punished for it. We are ever busy thinking about the misfortunes in our lives, but not how to resolve our problems or how to move into solutions. We allow the inner critic to take over our thoughts instead of building a healthy inner voice to do combat with the critic.

Your thoughts can hold you right in the bad situations that you want to desperately to get past in your life. The inner critic likes to keep you trapped in negativity because it means you stay stuck and consumed by your past. Take a moment now to realize that some of your repetitive bad thoughts are not realities in this moment. The bad incidences you keep thinking about are over and you have a choice to either move on in solution or allow yourself to become consumed by your own thinking.

Challenge yourself to work toward building a healthy inner voice so that when the inner critic comes out to do his work, the healthy inner voice is right there to rationalize the bad thoughts and move you forward in life. The healthy inner voice is there to remind you of the good person you are and the hard work you are doing to make your life a better place to be for yourself and those around you.

Feelings And Emotions

Feelings and emotions are caused by thoughts that linger in your mind. For example, you can't be angry without first having a bad thought or you can't feel stressed out without having stressful thoughts. There is a direct relationship between your thoughts and your reactions. In other words, when you think about your circumstances and allow your thoughts to run on automatic pilot, it is your thoughts that cause the problem not necessarily the circumstance itself. If you don't focus on a past circumstance, the circumstance will not exist. Use past experiences as a chance to learn and grow in your life. Do not dwell in bad experiences without purpose. Work toward the goal of getting out of a life of thoughts and victimization into a life of positive growth and new possibilities for yourself. You can work toward inner peace even if life is not exactly as you would like it to be.

Admitting Anger

Recognize and honor the fact that you are feeling angry. There is nothing wrong with admitting anger. In fact, it is admirable to accept your feelings and take responsibility for them. It takes honesty and an inner directed person to know when they are feeling angry and move toward solution without acting out in bad behavior. If you can't admit or recognize your anger, you won't be very successful in controlling it.

Assignment For The week

Take a full week to practice this chapter

Keep writing about your angry episodes and determine if it is truly anger or a different emotion you could be feeling.

Evaluate the strength of your anger and try not to put yourself in situations that can cause strong anger.

Make a plan to avoid situations that cause you to have strong anger.

Think about the following questions:

Are you focusing on your feelings and emotions?

How do you display your anger?

Can you get your anger under your own control quickly?

If you aren't experiencing anger, what else could it be?

What good things happened to you during the week? What did you like about your week/day? What worked for you today? What do you like about your life? What do you like about yourself?

Key point: Anger styles are learned behaviors. Learning to manage anger is a skill that has to be learned in adulthood. You were not born knowing anger management techniques, but there is not excuse for you to not learn them now.

Key point: You already know that warning signs have a purpose for you to sit up and take notice so that your anger will not escalate out of control. You also know that anger can grow out of control very quickly if you do not pay attention to your behaviors and warning signs. Be aware of the signs and pay attention to what your body and behavior are telling you!

Key Point: If you stay in your thoughts, you will stay in your past. If you become proactive in looking for ways to make yourself happier as an adult you will live in the present. Bad things do happen in childhood and life in general. However, right now, today in this moment, they are only your thoughts. Becoming a proactive inner directed person lies within your own thinking.

Key Point: Feelings and emotions are caused by thoughts that linger in your mind.

Chapter 5

Relax!

- Everyone experiences warning signs of anger at low levels. Learning to recognize your warning signs early will help you to keep your anger under control.
- No one can force you to have bad behavior when you are angry.
- You have a choice in how you handle your own anger.
- Surprise, fear and anger cause similar physical responses.
- Taking a brief moment to distinguish between surprise, fear and anger will help you to stay in control of your behavior.
- The way you respond to anger was not learned over night. It will take time and practice to learn healthy new ways to manage your anger.

The Foundations Of Anger Management

Let's do a brief recap and evaluate where you are at in the anger management process. At this point, you should be thinking about and be able to perform the following foundations of anger management:

- Accept responsibility of your anger.
- Realize and admit that you have a problem with anger.
- Understand that only you can control your own anger.
- Understand that you need to continue practicing what you are learning on a daily basis in order for anger management to be successful.
- Recognize when you are angry/frustrated/stressed.
- Begin to evaluate threats (fear, anger, surprise) and decide how to act responsibly.
- Review your journal and find patterns of where and when you experience anger, evaluate the intensity of your anger and develop a plan to help you avoid those situations.

Where Do I Go From Here?

For the past few weeks you have been practicing the basic foundations of anger management. Due to your hard work and becoming more proactive in your life I am confident that you are recognizing when you are experiencing the emotion of anger and repetitive negative thoughts. You should also be identifying other emotions that can quickly tip you over the edge into anger if you don't intervene with healthy solutions. Recognizing anger and the behavior that goes along with it is a HUGE accomplishment in anger management and is very necessary in the process of change. If you can't recognize it; you can't change it. Realizing that there are areas of your life in need of your attention is the starting point of exploring choice and freedom.

Give yourself a quick evaluation by using the anger management check up points at the beginning of this chapter. Are you experiencing success in the foundations of anger management? If you feel as though you are ready to move on and learn more possibilities of a healthier life style; keep moving through the book. If you are still having problems recognizing your emotions or having problems with a commitment to anger management; keep your focus in Chapters One-Four. Don't move on in the program until you are comfortable knowing what you need to change in your behavior or implement into your life to become successful in managing your anger. This isn't a race to see how quickly you get to the end of the book. This is about you creating real change in your life. Real change takes time, dedication, commitment, perseverance, desire, hard work…but you already know that.

The first four chapters of this workbook are probably some of the toughest for most of you because you are just getting started in the anger management process and beginning your process of change. You are just beginning to look at your behaviors and emotions which is a very tough task in the process of change. Even though we are moving forward in a different direction in Chapter Five, you will still need to be practicing and focusing on the previous chapters and the work you have completed in those chapters. Practice and keep your techniques fresh in your mind everyday as you move toward the Action Stage of change.

The second part of this anger management program is about living in solutions and finding ways to move forward in your life from a fresh and positive perspective. By switching your focus to coping through relaxation in this chapter and other solution focused techniques in upcoming chapters, you are adding yet another layer to your anger management foundation. I think you will find the next part of the anger management program exciting, challenging, scary, eye opening, and most importantly you will be finding yourself taking real control in your life.

Relaxation Techniques

This chapter is going to shift gears from behavioral monitoring to learning new ways of relaxing yourself mentally and physically. These techniques will not produce real results if you use them only occasionally or only when you are feeling angry. Just as committed as you have been to your anger treatment plan in Chapters One-Four by monitoring your behavior you must now add to your anger treatment plan and become committed to practicing relaxation techniques. Your anger treatment plan requires that you implement a relaxation technique at least once per day. Try each of the relaxation techniques to see which one works best for you and then implement it into your daily life.

Deep Breathing

Your breathing and heart rate both increase when you become emotionally aroused. You can learn to reverse these increases by deliberately slowing your breathing and relaxing your muscles.

One of the easiest and most convenient ways to relax your body is through slow, deep breaths. Deep breathing is convenient because you can do it anywhere, at any time, at work, shopping or wherever you feel anger creeping up and the beauty of it is that no one will know that you are practicing a relaxation technique. Breathing in and out slowly and deeply at the first signs of anger/frustration/stress will help you to relax and keep your emotions under your own control.

Deep breathing does not happen automatically. Deep breathing requires concentration and practice to find your own rate, rhythm and pace. Try to breathe in slowly and deeply. Count to four as you breathe in, and then breathe out slowly counting to four. Develop a routine that will help you to remember to practice deep breathing several times a day. You could do one set of deep breathing in the morning when you first wake up, the next set at an afternoon break and the third set when you lie down in bed right before you go to sleep.

Practice by taking three deep, steady breaths in a row. Try *not* to breathe in and out rapidly because you may hyperventilate and become dizzy. Breathe deeply to the count of four and exhale slowly to the count of four, in and out three times and you will feel your body start to relax. The more you practice this technique, the more proficient you will be when you really need to calm yourself in times of stress and anger. It sounds so simple doesn't it? It is simple, but you need to actually do the deep breathing to experience the benefits.

Think of some examples when deep breathing could help you deescalate your anger.

Examples:

- Standing in long lines in shopping centers.
- When you can't find a parking place and you have already driven around the lot 3 times.
- When your desk is piled 3 feet high and you see more work on the way.
- During a job interview.
- When you drive away from a drive through window and discover that they gave you the wrong food.

Now it's your turn. Think about times when you could use deep breathing as a means of relaxation.

Deep breathing could help me manage my anger when I:

_____

_____

_____

The hundreds of little stressors that come up on a daily basis can mount up to big and out of control anger if you are not catching yourself and intervening with a healthy solution. Try deep breathing during your stressful situations as a means of relaxation. Make time in your day to practice deep breathing techniques three times a day as an exercise and as part of your treatment plan. Not only will the relaxation techniques in this chapter help you to relax, they will enable you to think and respond more appropriately. When your mind is clear and relaxed you are able to concentrate on making good behavioral choices.

Muscle Relaxation

Anger frequently manifests itself in the form of muscle tension. Many of you probably feel most of your anger tension in your upper back and neck.

In order to practice muscle relaxation you will need to find a quite place where you can be alone and you won't experience any interruptions in the relaxation process.

If you are using your bedroom turn down the lights, lie down on your bed and try to clear your mind. It may take you a few moments to clear your head of thoughts and stressful situations that occurred throughout your day. Be patient in clearing your thoughts. You need to have a clear mind to concentrate on your relaxation process.

After you have cleared your mind and begin to feel relaxed, start at the top of your head and concentrate on relaxing the muscles of your head and face. For right now only think about relaxing your head and face. Let the muscles of your face relax and the muscles around your mouth droop.

After you have accomplished muscle relaxation around your head and face, think about the muscles in your neck. Let the tension and stressors drain out of your neck, let your neck melt into the pillow.

Now take your focus to your left shoulder and let it relax into the bed, picture the relaxation going from your shoulder down your left arm and through your hand. Hold the feeling of relaxation for a moment and then go over to the right shoulder and do the same thing starting with your shoulder and letting the relaxation go down through your right hand. Hold the feeling of relaxation.

Next, think about the muscles of your abdomen and back. Try not to hold yourself up from the bed, let yourself fall into it. Breathe in and out calmly with the same rhythm.

74

Concentrate on your lower back and hips. Relax… breathe and let the feelings of tension leave your body as you sink further into the mattress.

Focus on your buttocks, let everything go. Try not to hold any tension in your buttocks and lower back, let your body span out on the bed, you don't need to hold yourself up.

Picture the muscles of your left leg. Let the stress and tension leave from your thigh, down through your calf and out your left foot. Feel your left leg sink into the bed. Now picture the muscles of your right leg and let the stress leave your thigh, down through your calf and out your right foot.

If at any time you feel that you are tensing up any of the muscles that were relaxed, go back and try to relax them again. If you are not sure if you are relaxing a certain muscle, tense it up and then let it go. Feel the difference between a tense muscle and a relaxed one. Once you are completely relaxed, try to stay in the relaxed state for about 20 minutes or longer if needed.

The challenge for most people using muscle relaxation is trying to focus only on the relaxation techniques. The more you practice muscle relaxation, the more you will feel relaxed at the end of your session. The more you practice relaxation the easier it will be to clear your mind and stay focused in your process.

One huge benefit of relaxation is that it prepares you to finish out the rest of your day in a much more pleasant place. When you practice relaxation techniques you are a proactive participant in your own life and you are finding ways to live in solution. Not only will you benefit from feeling more relaxed, your loved ones will also benefit from you taking the time to relax the stressors out of your day. Just like anger affects everyone in its proximity, so will positive living and feeling good about yourself.

Getting In The Game At Home

What is the first thing you like to do when you get home from a long stressful day?

Many people like to come home and unwind from a stressful day before they can start activities with friends and family. It isn't easy to just shift gears from a high stress day and throw yourself into a home full of activities. Some proactive people like to take a block of alone time to bathe, read the paper, book or listen to music. Everyone can benefit from a planned break or time in their day to enjoy something by themselves. If you are a stay at home parent or work out of your home you too need time to yourself to relax and unwind from stress. Everyone deserves time alone to clear your mind and relax.

If you are not sure if you could benefit from this time out or skeptical of the idea… try it. A short half hour break could mean the difference between healthy behavior and acting out using bad behavior. Throughout the years, many clients have told me that one of their biggest stressors is coming home to activities and trying to jump in and join the game while they are still stressed from the first half of their day. Make it your priority to set aside time when you can be free to do whatever relaxation activity or hobby you enjoy. Your time out might include exercise, reading, ceramics, needlepoint, working on the car, landscaping or whatever activity allows you to free your mind to relax.

When I advocate time out periods for relaxation and enjoyment in my anger management sessions people can't wait to tell me, "I am too busy; I don't have a half hour to spend on something for myself." Are you really too busy to find a half hour in your **24 hour day** to make a better life for yourself? *Everyone* has at least a half hour in their day to get healthy. Adult breaks are much needed and very necessary to reduce stress. Relaxation is a part of healthy living. Make a commitment to schedule your relaxation time and if you can keep the same time slot every day for either a relaxation technique or any activity that brings you joy. This is all part of becoming proactive in your life and living in solutions that work best for you.

There is one small catch to a relaxation time away. Before you take your relaxation time out, you just cannot go away, out of sight and not let others know you are taking time alone to recover from your day. Explain to your loved ones that you need time to unwind from work and that you can't wait to spend time with them, but first you need a half hour to unwind before joining home activities. You might want to have an agreement with your family/partner/spouse ahead of time such as: between 5:30 and 6:00 pm I need to engage in my time out activity alone on a daily basis.

There may be others in your household who could benefit from a time out, but won't be able to take time away without your help. Make a plan ahead of time to allow everyone the chance to relax and de-stress from the activities of their day. When you plan to relax and enjoy your life, you are living in solution and being a proactive participant in your own life. Taking care of yourself requires that you first make a plan and then follow up on your plan with an action.

My planned time out activities:

_____

_____

Another Technique, Imagine That!

Relaxing Imagery

Have you ever had a pleasant thought of something that made you happy and automatically a smile came over your face and you felt joy? Do you have a thought or pleasant image in mind that makes you smile? Think of something that makes you happy and try to imagine it now. Try to think of something calm and peaceful.

Close your eyes and imagine yourself in that peaceful calm place that makes you happy and try to see, feel, smell, taste and touch it. Let your mind drift and try to re-experience the happy occasion. You just practiced relaxing imagery!

Leah

Leah experiences numerous episodes of anger and stress in her high pressure job of CEO of a major construction company. Many times throughout her busy day Leah feels like exploding, but before she lets her anger get out of control she practices a relaxing technique she learned in this workbook.

The relaxation technique Leah found works the best for her is trying to imagine her self somewhere else in a more pleasant place. The place Leah likes to envision is when she and her husband took a trip to Hawaii on their last anniversary. Leah found total paradise on the Big Island.

Leah imagines:

Sight: Leah can see herself on top of a mountain looking down at the ocean waves lapping at the shoreline.

Smell: She smells the aroma of some of the most exotic flowers she has ever smelled lingering in the air.

Hearing: She experiences almost complete silence with only the waves from the ocean.

Touch: The warm breeze blows the heavy smell of coconuts and flowers so much so that she feels as though she is holding one right in her very hands.

Taste: The aroma of the flowers mixing with a hint of coconut is almost edible.

It's Your Turn Now

Try to imagine a pleasant event that will take you away from your stressful thoughts.

My relaxing scene: _____

_____

Sight: _____

Smell: _____

Hearing: _____

Touch: _____

Taste: _____

Practice Makes Perfect

Practice each of the three relaxation techniques to see which one works best for you. You may find that one technique works better than another or maybe you will need to combine all three to help you relax.

Remember, the main purpose of a relaxation technique is to keep you calm and to help you plan ways to control your anger and keep it manageable.

The relaxation technique that works best for me is:

_____
_____
_____

Fun

By now I am sure you have figured out that anger management is really more than simply managing your anger. It is about planning and developing an anger plan so that your life becomes manageable and under your own control. Anger management is about implementing positive solutions so that you are not only focusing on the serious issues that need to be changed, but also learning lightheartedness and implementing fun. Part of your anger treatment plan in this chapter is to implement fun into your life. Maybe some of you have abandoned fun and don't even remember what the meaning of fun really is anymore.

What Is Fun?

- Relaxation (you just learned the techniques) and stress reduction.
- Sense of humor and lightheartedness.
- A hobby.
- Physical exercise.
- Leisure time where you have absolutely nothing to do.
- A recess from the responsibilities of life.
- Making time for yourself to do exactly what you want to do.

What Are Barriers To Having Fun?

- An overly serious attitude.
- Poorly managed time and always rushing yourself to the next task.
- Too busy to even think of having fun.

- Lack of permission from yourself, partner, family, spouse.
- Not being receptive to having fun or implementing fun activities.
- Never really learned how to have fun in early life.

Beliefs That Are Barriers To Having Fun

- It is selfish to have fun.
- It takes away time from more serious activities of life.
- Having fun takes a lot of money.
- Feeling guilty doing nothing or just plain relaxing.
- Not having time for fun.
- The thought that having fun is a waste of time.

Make a list of ways you would like to implement fun into your life:

_____

_____

_____

_____

Examples of having fun could be: having a picnic, taking a walk, cooking a dinner, a long bath with candles, playing sports, sleeping in, having a party for no reason....

In your journal, I would like you to make a column to add in a stress reduction or relaxation technique at least once per day and another column of fun activities you implement into your daily life. Anger management is about finding yourself, being kind to yourself and making time for yourself. Use your imagination and have fun with it!

Assignment For The Week

Take a full week to practice this chapter.

Continue writing in your journal and each time you get angry, write the techniques you chose to calm your angry feelings.

Try to choose a relaxation technique that works well for you and be dedicated in using it. Be creative and think of your own techniques.

Relaxation is good for your physical well being and also has a positive side effect of helping you to stop focusing on being angry. Relaxing will give you time to think about the situation that has upset you and some fresh solutions to the problems you are facing.

Set a time out for relaxation. Relaxing is a must in your anger management treatment plan.

Think about the following questions:

What are the foundations of anger management?

What relaxation techniques work best for you?

When do you find yourself having to use relaxation techniques?

Remember to look for your positive progress. Congratulate yourself when you do something well. Recognize your achievements. This is a tough process, but you are here and you are doing it.

What good things happened to you during the week? What did you like about your week/day? What worked for you today? What do you like about your life? What do you like about yourself?

Key Point: Your breathing and heart rate both increase when you become emotionally aroused. You can learn to reverse these increases by deliberately slowing your breathing and relaxing your muscles.

Key Point: Part of your anger plan is to implement fun into your life.

Key Point: Everyone deserves time alone to clear your mind and relax.

Key Point: Every day includes 24 hours. There is at least a ½ hour for you to have time to practicing relaxation and implementing fun in your life.

Chapter 6

Negative Coping Strategies

- You have 3 relaxation techniques: deep breathing, muscle relaxation and relaxing imagery.
- One relaxation technique may work better than another or you could use all 3 techniques together. Practicing will help you become proficient in the technique that works best for you.
- One of the easiest and most convenient ways to relax your body is through deep breathing.
- Small stressors can mount up to big anger if it is not controlled early in the game.
- Identifying anger takes conscious thought and practice to unlearn impulsive, explosive behavior.
- Everyone benefits from time alone to relax and unwind.

Talking To Yourself

When you repeat negative thoughts over and over again, you are experiencing repetitive negative self-talk and you are actually practicing negativity. Practicing negativity is equivalent to practicing unhappiness. Repetitive unhappiness and negative self-talk, left unattended, leads to unpleasant emotions, stressful physical responses, and reinforces an already in place inner critic. Negativity allows anger to fester, causes your anger to escalate and in turns lowers your self esteem.

As humans, we are constantly thinking and trying to make sense out of our lives. We think about the past, present, future, what we did wrong, guilt and shame, but rarely do we think of solutions to aid in building and reinforcing a healthy inner voice to squash the inner critic. Rather than build a healthy inner voice, we tend to reinforce the negative inner critic because he is most familiar to us. Over the years and with all of our practice we have come to know the inner critic well. We are familiar with what he is going to say and we can always count on him to be right there to help us think and lower our self esteem whenever we allow him to take over our thoughts.

You might be thinking to yourself that it is not always possible to stay mentally alert and monitor thoughts every moment of your waking life. It *is* difficult to monitor your every thought, but it is critical that you monitor and catch your negative thoughts when they first start so that you can stop them move into a positive solution immediately.

Your thoughts cause a feeling, which in turn affects your actions/reactions. Remember from previous chapters; first there is a thought, then comes a feeling and then eventually comes the bad behavior if you are not paying close attention to your thought process. In other words, remember that you can't feel angry without having angry or negative thoughts first just like you can't feel happy and joyful without thinking happy and positive thoughts. There is an absolute link between thinking and feeling. You need to catch yourself thinking!

I am pretty sure that you have heard the old saying, "you are what you think you are." If you think you are a bad person because you feel angry, then you will react and feel like a bad person with anger. The process starts out by you manufacturing your own bad thought which in turn creates a bad feeling that can quickly get you into trouble if you don't intervene in your thought process. If you leave the bad feelings unattended and continue to allow the inner critic to guide you into how you should think and feel, you will eventually move into unwanted bad behaviors. And, you will continue feeling badly about yourself which in turn creates low self esteem and only serves to build up the inner critic and make him a driving force in your life.

Inner Critic

Are you wondering about this inner critic? Who is he? Are you curious of where he comes from? The inner critic is born in childhood when your parents teach you "right from wrong" "good from bad," which behaviors are allowed in your family, and what is tolerable and acceptable in the family unit. When you do something that is not tolerated by your family, you may have been punished by spanking, with holding of affection, or isolation. In essence, you were made to feel like a bad person. When you are a child, these experiences can be very deeply felt. As you begin to grow up, you retain what you learned in "right and wrong" and those scars wound the self esteem. This is where the critic starts. If you do something bad or make a mistake, the inner critic reminds you of what you already may believe about yourself engrained from years ago.

We all have battle scars from childhood; however, as adults we need to recognize the scars and come to the understanding that we don't have to live in the scars or bad feelings of yesterday today. You don't have to rely on the inner critic to tell you what a bad person you are or how you didn't do something "right." If you continue to feed the negative inner critic with self defeating thoughts, you will only reinforce negativity in your life and you will stay stuck in your emotions and in your past.

Rather than fuel the inner critic, let's work toward a sense of self love and self esteem. Don't cover up the love for yourself by insecure thoughts and doubt. Strive to understand that you are a good and worthwhile person. As an adult, you can make a choice to put a stop to the negative thoughts that pop up in your mind and come to the realization that your thoughts are… simply thoughts. Remember, your thoughts are not necessarily the reality of your situation.

In order to move on in your life in solution you must catch yourself thinking. Spend this next week monitoring your critical self talk. Write in your journal about your thoughts and your critical statements.

Example:

Time	Critical Statement
8:30	I think my friends are sick of me.
9:30	How could I have done something so stupid?
11:00	My house is a constant mess.

You get the flavor of the exercise. Try to catch yourself having negative, critical thoughts and decide if you are thinking in the present moment or pulling from past history. Are your thoughts reality? Are they rational? Evaluate your thoughts to determine if they are accurate.

Be aware that sometimes your thoughts can also shift one step further into self protection while reinforcing the inner critic. Remember, you don't want to defend your thoughts. You want to catch yourself having thoughts and then engage your rational brain to think them through and make sense out of them.

Examples of self protective and defensive repetitive self-talk:

"I didn't get the raise because my boss doesn't like me."

"My work performance is perfect, my boss is the jerk."

"I bend over backwards for this company. Everything I do is for the company's good."

"From now on, it's all about me. When I go to work I am going to take it easy like everyone else."

"Even though this is the best job I have ever had, if I find out other employees got raises, I am out of here!"

"No one appreciates the work I do around this house. From now on, everyone will do their own!"

Don't try to defend yourself and your thoughts because it will only serve to build the inner critic and you will stay stuck in negativity. Instead, notice your self defeating thoughts and try to turn them around into more rational positive thoughts. Defending negative thoughts will keep you in the negative spiral of the inner critic. Try to view each situation with neutrality and do not jump to conclusions. Become aware and of your thoughts and try to put a stop to run away critical thinking.

Stop your thoughts, take a few deep breaths and allow your rational brain and your healthy voice to make decisions and form beliefs. When you allow your run away thoughts to become self protective and defensive you actually begin practicing negative self scripts.
Negative self-scripts play a huge part in your decisions, they influence your choices and effect your effort to change.

What Are Negative Self Scripts?

- Negative beliefs you have about yourself and of which you remind yourself daily.
- Negative remarks you say about yourself and influence your behaviors and beliefs.
- Negative self images of your body, looks, weight which you think influence your presentation of self to others.
- Negative stories about your past behavior and failures that influence your current conduct.
- Feelings of guilt for real or imagined wrongs you have committed.
- Feelings of inferiority.

When you repeat the negative self scripts over and over in your mind you run the risk of developing low self esteem and the inability to see any value in your own life. Negative self talk immobilizes you from taking risks in life, prevents you from making change and freezes you into negative thinking patterns. Repeating negative self scripts and self talk over and over only leads you to see the world and you life in a negative light.

The more you make yourself aware of negative self-talk, the more you will start to recognize it quickly. The more you practice monitoring your thoughts, the more you will be able to recognize and stop negative self-talk before it interferes with your decisions. The more you practice catching your thinking, the better acquainted you will become with your inner critic and the easier it will become to stop him and work toward building a healthy inner voice.

Different Types Of Negative Self-Talk

Negative thinking is a habit that is formed throughout a lifetime (negative inner critic) and is very difficult to break without your conscious effort. Negative coping techniques reveal only the difficulties in a situation, cause you to postpone life's enjoyment and don't allow you to see that you have choices. You may be thinking that your life isn't always perfect and there will be times when negative thinking is unavoidable... and you could be right. There will be times in life when negative thinking will match your circumstances, but my goal for you is to recognize your negative thinking, become conscious of negative thought patterns and learn to let them go or find solutions to pull you out of negative thoughts and situations. When you learn to clear your mind of negative thoughts, your solutions and choices will be much clearer and you become free to move into more healthy solutions.

As you quiet your mind from negative thinking, the extra stress and panic your thoughts cause will fade and you will be able to better operate with a rational thought process. It will take time and a lot of practice to catch yourself in the act of negative thinking. It will also take time and practice to create new habits of thinking in the present rather than thinking in the past. Study the following types of negative self talk/thoughts and try to determine which thinking patterns you may use when you are confronted with negative thoughts and feelings.

Filtering:

If you are *filtering* your thoughts, you are disregarding everything except the most negative aspects of a situation. When you filter your thoughts, you focus *only* on the negative aspects of a situation and exclude any positive elements or options. Filtering makes you feel helpless and hopeless. When you filter, you dwell only on the negative and everything is bad.

Filtering:
- Focuses only on the negative points of a situation.
- Excludes any positive options.
- Discounts any type of positive coping.

Examples of filtering negative thoughts and self-talk:

"This is just awful."
"There is nothing that I can do to help this situation."
"Everything in my life is ruined because of this."
"Nobody cares that I am this miserable."

Black And White:

If you are using *black and white* self talk you are using "all or nothing" thinking. It's either all very good or it's all very bad. There is no middle ground or gray area. You do not give yourself options.

Black and White:

- Severely limits your options.
- Only allows a one sided view.
- Filters out the positive and the negative thought process takes over.

Examples of black and white thoughts and self-talk:

"It's either my way or the highway."
"Either you make it right or don't make it all."
"That's what I think about it and you can't change my mind!"

Over Generalizing

If you are using *over generalizing* self-talk you are taking the outcome of one situation and applying it to all other situations you experience. In other words, if you had a very bad experience while you were shopping at a certain store you will apply that same bad situation to every shopping trip.

Over generalizing:
- Causes incorrect and over generalized conclusions.
- Uses words such as: none, never, always.
- Takes one incident and applies it to all other situations.

Examples of over generalized thoughts and self-talk:

"I *never* get to do the things that I enjoy."
"I *always* do all the work around here."
"People *never* seem to enjoy having me around."
"I will *never* go back to that mall again!"

Mind Reading

If you are using *mind reading*, you are making assumptions about what others are thinking without actually knowing for sure. You do the thinking for them.

Mind reading:

- Makes you realize that your assumptions are actually facts.
- Makes you act out on assumptions without ever really knowing the facts.
- Reads into others thoughts for hidden messages and meanings.

Examples of mind reading thoughts and self-talk:

"I know what my boss is thinking about my work performance."
"He doesn't ask me to go out with him because I know I am not his type."
"The reason the clerk isn't waiting on me is because he thinks I can't afford it."

Can you identify with any of the negative self-talk examples you just read? Do you filter? Tend to over generalize situations? Do you think there is only one way or the highway?

My negative self talk involves:

_____
_____
_____

Pick And Chose Your Thoughts

Quite simply; your thoughts determine the way you feel about yourself and the world in general. The best part of being in control of your thoughts is realizing you *are* in charge of your own thinking and you *are* capable of changing your attitude. Rather than waiting for others to change and wasting your energy on what you can't control, you can spend the energy looking for ways to improve your own life and take control of your own circumstances.

Earlier in this chapter, we talked about the old saying "you are what you think you are." If we were to look at that saying a little closer we would realize that if you pay attention to happy thoughts; you are happy. If you pay attention to negative, anger provoking thoughts; you become angry and feel negative. When you develop a positive outlook; you become less defensive and the possibilities of the world reveal themselves. When you look for what's right in the world; you will find the positive things offered to you in your life. When you look on the world with a hopeful attitude; you will see hopeful things and experience the goodness of others.

Make a commitment to monitor your thoughts every day. At the very first sign that you are engaging in negative self-talk, catch yourself in the act and stop it immediately. Use your word/phrase to jolt you out of the negative self talk circle. Run away thoughts and rampant negative thoughts only serve to escalate your current anger and in some cases can even *cause* anger.

You are probably thinking…but my thoughts come to me automatically! What am I supposed to do? I can't control them! **FACT:** You *are* capable of roping in your thinking. You *do* have the power and control to stop and refocus your thoughts on to more positive and rational thinking when you take the time to notice your negative thought processes. If you can notice it; you *can* change it.

When you first start paying attention to your thoughts, you will be surprised to find out how often you actually experience negative thoughts without even realizing it. Writing in your journal will help you to monitor and keep track of your negative thoughts. By noticing a pattern in your thinking you will be able to see that negative thinking can play a huge part in your anger, stress and general feeling of being overwhelmed. When you are involved in negative thinking, you are not involved in the present moment or the positive aspects in your life.

Examples Of Negative Thinking:

Negative thought: "They only invited me to the party because they feel sorry for me."
Refocus: "They wouldn't invite someone into their home if they didn't like them."

Negative: "He only says he likes my proposal to look good in front of the other employees. He really hates it."
Refocus: "He must like my proposal because he has no problem telling people what he thinks!"

Negative: "She is pretending to like my dress, but deep down, I can tell she thinks I look fat in it."
Refocus: "She's right; I do look good in this dress."

Take The Challenge

When you are experiencing negative thoughts, ask yourself the following questions to guide your thinking:

- Do I have evidence for having these thoughts?
- Am I seeing the whole picture or only seeing what I want to see?
- How did I come to this conclusion?
- Is this the healthiest way to think about this situation?
- What are the true facts?

Asking yourself these questions will help lead your thoughts from the negative to the facts.

Changing Your Ways

If you find that you are using *filtering* as a negative coping behavior, you are probably "weeding out" everything except the bad or negative thoughts. Turn your thoughts and attention toward positive strategies and try not to focus only on the negative aspects of the situation. Treat every situation as a new and exciting experience. By changing your negative thoughts into positive you are making the choice to live in solution.

If you are using *black and white* thinking as a negative coping behavior, make an effort to get rid of the words: always, never, usually, none. No one "always" "never" "usually" does anything. If you are accusing someone of "always" being on the phone, rationalize your thoughts and ask yourself how can someone "always" be on the phone? "It seems like you are on the phone a lot" would be a more rational thought. There will always be more than two options or choices to any situation.

If you are using *over generalization* as a negative coping behavior, try to stick with the current situation and remind yourself to evaluate each situation independently of one another. Not all situations will have the same outcome no matter what your experiences were in the past. You have no way of predicting what will happen in the future. Try to stay away from statements about the future and live in today.

If you are using *mind reading* as a negative coping behavior, you need to throw out your crystal ball and stop thinking for other people. You will never be successful in guessing what others think or feel. Mind reading will lead you to inaccurate conclusions and unnecessary anger, stress and frustration. Shock yourself back into reality by concentrating only on the *known* facts.

Negative Self-Talk Example

Michael

Michael was applying for college for the very first time in his life at the age of 39. The college scheduled him to come in for placement testing on Monday morning. Having never been to college before, Michael was nervous and not really sure what to expect on his first visit. When he got to the college, there were about 20 other students in a big room waiting to take the same exam Michael was scheduled to take. Michael looked around the room at all the other students who were mostly recent high school graduates and thought they must be wondering what the heck *he* was doing there.

Michael's negative self-talk began to take over without him even noticing his thoughts. Even though the other students were not really judging or looking at Michael, he imagined them to be thinking poorly of him. He thought they must be wondering what a guy his age was doing there. He wondered if they were thinking that he dressed old fashioned or that his hair was out of style.

The more Michael thought about the other students the angrier he got. He imagined himself fist fighting with them and even asked one student, "What the hell are you looking at?" The student looked away in fear. Michael thought, "See, even at my age, I could take them all!" His thoughts quickly escalated into if the students were having those kinds of thoughts about him, what must the faculty be thinking about him? His heart was pounding so hard he could feel it in his ears all the way to the top of his head and down his shoulders. The back of his neck tightened and his face turned bright red. Michael decided to leave the test room and forget about getting a college education. To Michael, the stress wasn't worth a future advancement if he had to put up with his thoughts and feelings just to get there.

How did negative self-talk affect Michael? His anger may have started off (mild) thinking that the other students were looking at him but quickly escalated (irrational) all the way up to "I could take them all." (Aggression)

I wonder if Michael recognized that his anger was escalating. Do you think things would have worked out differently for Michael if he realized that he had the power and control to stop his negative thoughts? Did he see the warning signs? Can you see how quickly negative self-talk can spiral out of control and affect your behavior when you are not monitoring and rationalizing your thinking?

If you could ask Michael questions about his thoughts and emotions, what might you ask him?

- Do you really think that the students were judging you for being at the college?
- Did they really care about what you looked like or dressed like?
- Do you think the other students were thinking about fighting you simply because you are 39 years old?
- Do you think the other students may have been just as nervous as you and searching the crowd for a friendly face?
- Who suffered as a result of you leaving the school? What price did you pay for not pursuing your dreams of a college education?

Although Michael may have thought all of those things, do you think he was accurate in his thoughts? Negative self-talk usually starts out by making wrong assumptions, not sticking to the facts and escalates quickly out of control without your attention. Negative self talk can make anger go from mild to strong using only your own negative thoughts.

After reading about negative coping techniques (mind reading, black and white thinking, over generalizing), which techniques do you think Michael may have used at the college?

List all of the negative coping behaviors Michael used while at the college:

_____
_____
_____

Practice Thought Stopping With Michael

Negative: "I bet the other students are staring at me because they think I am too old to be here!"
STOP
Positive: "The other students don't even know me, they are probably nervous too."

Negative: "If the students think I am old, I can just imagine what the instructors are thinking!"
STOP
Positive: "I bet the instructors are going to like having someone my age in their class. They probably like that I am trying to improve myself at 39."

Negative: "I'll never get where I want to be in life because I do not have a college degree."
STOP
Positive: "I'm going to make another appointment at the college and this time I will finish the exams."

Let's try another example:

Holly

Holly was up for a big promotion at her job. She was happy to be considered for the position because her first thought was that she really did earn a step up in her career and she knew she was the best candidate. As the interviews drew near all she could think about was whether or not she was good enough or if she really had done her job as good as she could have. Did she really deserve this promotion or were they just being kind to her because she had worked there so long? The more she thought about it the more she started to think negatively about her job performance. She thought to herself: I remember when I could have stayed longer to work on the project. I think I could have handled my client better last month. Her head became filled with negativity and her inner critic took over the once confident and deserving employee. The more she thought, the more she realized that she really wasn't qualified for the job and who were they kidding to even be asking her?

Take a moment now and identify some of the negative coping skills Holly used getting ready for her promotional interview:

_____
_____
_____
_____

More Practice

Practice these 4 steps to wage the war on your negative self talk and irrational beliefs:

1. Be aware, realize (recognize) that you are having negative self- talk.
2. Stop the thoughts.
3. Stick to just the facts.
4. Change your negative self-talk around into positive self-talk.

Irrational Beliefs

Irrational beliefs are messages we send to ourselves that keep us from growing emotionally, hold us in negativity and keep the inner critic active. Irrational beliefs are:

- Self defeating ways of acting.
- Counter productive ways of thinking.

- Negative or pessimistic ways of viewing life experiences.
- Ways of thinking about ourselves that are out of context.
- Scripts we have in our heads about how life "should" be.
- Unproductive, unrealistic expectations.

Examples Of Irrational Beliefs

- I am worthless.
- I am powerless to change my life.
- I should not burden others with my problems or fears.
- I should just give up.
- I have way to many problems. More than anyone else in the world.
- I am stupid.
- No one cares about me or anyone else.
- I don't want to deal with anyone because I will only get hurt.
- Admitting to mistakes is a sign of failure and weakness.

If you feel as though you are constantly bombarded with negative, irrational beliefs you need to work on becoming immediately aware of your thoughts and turning those thoughts and beliefs around into positive self talk. Begin by knocking down the inner critic and start building a healthy inner voice.

Healthy Inner Voice

Building a healthy inner voice requires you to first catch yourself having self defeating thoughts started by the negative inner critic and then talking back to the negative inner critic with a healthy inner voice. Think of a thought stopping saying you can use to jolt you into rationalizing your thoughts. Remember in Chapter One when you chose a phrase or word to stop you from allowing your anger to escalate? Now I would like for you think of a word or phrase that you can use to stop the repetitive negative thoughts. Some examples might be: stop it, get off my back, stop this crap, stinkin thinkin, calm down, quiet down… your turn.

My thought stopping word or phrase:

_____

Pay attention to yourself and pick and chose your thoughts wisely. When you begin to experience negative thoughts you do have a choice. You can allow the negativity to continue or you can pull out your healthy inner voice to help you rationalize the negative thoughts. You can allow the inner critic to guide your life or you can pull out the healthy inner voice and work toward living in solution. Pay attention to your inner guide that you are developing in this anger management process and learn to trust your wisdom. You have wisdom; you just need to *know* that you have inner wisdom and learn to rely on it.

The goal is to render the inner critic useless and to meet your needs without relying on him to remind you of your negative thoughts and feelings. The goal is to boost your self esteem by pulling out the healthy inner voice to do combat each time the negative inner critic wants to take control of your life. The goal is to realize there are positive and negative things going on in your life every day and that you can chose to focus on the positive instead of the negative. You are making the choice to look for what's *right* in every situation and living in solution rather than concentrating on the negative and what's wrong with your life. Your quality of thinking determines the quality of your life.

Instead of concentrating on the negative self scripts and the negative self talk begin by using positive self affirmations.

What Are Positive Self Affirmations?

- Positive self scripts that you give yourself to replace the negative self scripts.
- Take personal responsibility for your emotional and physical health.
- Let go of the negative emotional baggage you have been carrying around.
- Give yourself permission to grow, change and make a better life for yourself.
- Resolve feelings and emotions from the past so that you can face the present with a clear view.
- Let go of people who drain you and never give back.
- Recognize your rights and equality in life.
- Live to your fullest potential.

Statements Of Positive Change

- I like myself.
- I will control my temper today,
- I will grow emotionally stronger every day.
- I will smile more today.
- I will feel less guilt today and every day.
- I will manage my time better today.
- I will take a risk today.
- I will face my fears.
- I will lose weight.
- I will quit smoking.
- I will exercise and eat right.
- I will challenge myself to change today.
- I will do a better job at work today.
- I am a winner.
- I am responsible for my own feelings.
- I deserve to relax more.
- I am a capable human being.
- I deserve to have my rights recognized and honored.

- I am able to handle any problem I face.
- There are beautiful things and people in my life.

Your statements of positive change: (I can, I am, I will)

_____
_____
_____
_____
_____

We started this chapter off on the topic of negativity and I would like to end the chapter getting you ready for positive solutions and positive change. I would like for you to start thinking this week about building a healthy relationship with your inner self through inward listening. Understanding the statements below will help you to build your healthy inner voice, learn inner wisdom and raise your self-esteem.

- All feelings are okay and part of being human and alive.
- When you repeatedly block your emotions or you don't listen to your inner voice you risk acting out your emotions inappropriately.
- When you begin to listen to your inner voice and honor the message you begin to trust yourself and you will build true confidence.
- When you understand your emotions you are more capable of meeting your own needs.
- When you listen to and rationalize your inner thoughts you are taking control and the negative thoughts and feelings will begin to diminish.
- After time and practice the whole process of inward listening will become more natural and you will be guiding yourself from your own positive thoughts and good self esteem.

Assignment For The Week

Continue writing in your journal. Write about your anger, critical thoughts and solutions you use to stop negative thinking.

Think about your own negative self-talk and decide which of the techniques mentioned in this chapter you use when thinking negatively.

Think of all your options and ways to change the negative thoughts into positive thoughts. Make the effort to live in solution.

When you start to experience negative self-talk, STOP and become aware that you are having negative self-talk.

Think about the following questions:

94

How do you talk to yourself?

Do you filter, use black and white thinking, over generalize, or try to mind read?

How do you stop your negative self talk?

What are your thought stopping techniques?

Remember to look for your positive progress. Congratulate yourself when you do something well. Recognize your achievements. This is a tough process, but you are here and you are doing it.

What good things happened to you during the week? What did you like about your week/day? What worked for you today? What do you like about your life? What do you like about yourself?

Even if you are justified in feeling angry about a situation, it is not okay to simply attack the target of your anger. Just as importantly as not attacking is to stop the negative inner critic and put an end to repetitious negative producing thoughts.

Key point: Not all thoughts need to be entertained. Many thoughts are based on low self esteem, low moods, fear, hurt and many more emotions can cause negative thoughts. Pick and chose your thoughts wisely.

Key point: The goal of anger management is to live in your life today and not continually reminisce about how difficult past situations have been for you. The goal is to render the inner critic useless and to meet your needs without relying on him to remind you of your negative thoughts and feelings.

Key point: The goal anger management is to boost your self esteem by pulling out the healthy inner voice to do combat each time the negative inner critic wants to take control of your life.

Key point: The goal of anger management is to realize there are positive and negative things going on in your life and you can chose to focus on the positive instead of the negative. You are making the choice to look for what's *right* in every situation and living in solution rather than concentrating on the negative.

Key point: Pick and chose your thoughts wisely. When you begin to experience negative thoughts you have a choice. You can allow the negativity to continue or you can pull out your healthy inner voice to help you rationalize the negative thoughts

Chapter 7

Turning It All Around

- Negative self-talk can be dangerous especially when you are already angry.
- Negative ways to handle anger could be: negative comments, sarcasm, withdrawing from situations, temper tantrums, denying your feelings.
- Sticking with just the facts will help you decrease your negative thoughts.
- Recognize you are experiencing negative self-talk.
- Try to stop it negative self talk so that it does not spiral out of control.
- Stick to the facts.
- Change the negative into positive thoughts.
- You are in control of your own thoughts and behaviors.

Positive Self-Talk

You learned in the last chapter that thinking is a natural part of being human. In fact, you now know that thinking is so natural that it is easy to forget when you are even doing it! When you become proactive in your life and you begin monitoring your thought processes you will be shocked at how often your thoughts actually turn toward negativity. Your next anger management challenge in this chapter is to begin monitoring your thoughts, constantly checking for negativity and making a plan to move into positive solution.

The idea here is to break the old habit of negative thinking and replace it with positive self talk. The easiest way to think of positive self-talk is simply to think of it as the exact opposite of negative self-talk. While it might sound easy to "just turn the negative thought into a positive thought", the hardest part is in catching yourself in the act of having the negative thought. Negative self-talk is usually automatic and most people don't even realize they are experiencing it until the negativity causes a physical reaction or an act of uncontrolled anger. Remember, first there is usually a thought (negative), then comes a feeling followed by a reaction.

Important Point from Chapter Six: At the very first sign of your thoughts becoming repetitive and negative the goal is to get your conscious thought stopping mechanism to kick in and go to work. Conscious thought stopping involves putting an end to negative messages as soon as you realize you are experiencing them.

First, as soon as you notice an uncomfortable feeling or emotion; tell yourself to stop physically and mentally to check in with your emotions. Second, ignore or avoid focusing on and repeating your negative thoughts. Third, refocus your mind toward healthy functioning thoughts based on the truth and reality. When you free your mind of negativity, you are freeing yourself up to see the positives in life. When you become more proactive in your life, you become more productive and full of energy. When you become positive, you will become less defensive and less ready to see the "bad." If you think positive and hopeful, you will see your life as positive and hopeful.

It is important to realize that your thinking can create great joy in your life or great pain and suffering. To get out of the negative loop, you have to remember you are the one doing the thinking and you are also the one who can either allow yourself to sit in negatively and repetitive bad thoughts or you can become proactive and change your thinking.

Tips For Changing Your Self-Talk

- Try to catch yourself saying or thinking negative thoughts, words or ideas.
- Say *no* or *stop* to negative words, thoughts and ideas.
- Be careful not to exaggerate the situation or your feelings.
- Try not to use words such as: never, always, none. (He never does what I ask him to do. She is always on the telephone).
- Think positive, hopeful thoughts.
- Think about the things that are *right* in your life.

Assignment: In your journal, make a list of positive thoughts regarding your life and read them aloud to yourself (I am a caring and nice person. I have a wonderful family and friends. I like myself, I represent myself well in the world, I have a good life).
Try to critique yourself fairly in your list of positive thoughts and remember that *everything* can't be all negative in your life. Think of your positive attributes. (I don't look so good in this green shirt, but I do look great in the blue one. I can't get my work done as quickly as my partner, but I do a better job).

By making this list, you are beginning the process of replacing irrational with rational thoughts, replacing the negatives with positives, and replacing the bad thoughts with the truth. Remind yourself that negative self-talk will not fix the problem; it will only make it worse. Negative self-talk will keep you negative, positive self talk will help you to live in the truth and find happiness.

Make It Easy

When you first begin to change your thinking process, you may struggle in trying to exchange your negative thoughts for positive replacements. Thought stopping is very difficult, but you are very capable of controlling your own thinking, but first you have to recognize and become aware of your thoughts.

Get proactive. Make your thought stopping or positive self-talk personal to you by thinking of a saying, a word or an image that you can quickly remember when you are having negative thoughts.

Some people visualize a stop sign or simply say **stop** out loud to jolt their brain from having a negative thought to a positive one. Thinking of your personal image or a phrase will help you to become aware of repetitive negative thoughts and will move your thoughts toward positive thinking. The idea here is to help you transform your negative self-talk and thoughts into positive self-talk by creating a break in your thoughts.

Have some fun and break out your creative skills. For my thought stopping technique, I think of a star. Have you ever walked out into your backyard on a clear crispy night and look up to see a sky full of beautiful twinkling stars? Not only is it an easy word for me to remember, it is also a very pleasant vision to imagine.

STAR

S = Stop. Stop all thoughts for a moment and take a mental break.

T = Think. Think about why I am having negative thoughts.

A = Act. Act in ways to stop or calm my anger.

R = Review. Review the situation to see if it needs further attention.

It's All about You

It's all about what works best for you. What may work well for other people might not work for you at all. You need to put time and practice into learning what techniques work best for you. Success in anger management is all about learning to manage your anger in a way that is personalized to fit your life. Take the time now to think of some thoughts or images that could work to help you re-focus your negative thoughts into positive possibilities.

Positive self-talk motivates you to think in positive and it implements change. Negative self- talk keeps you right there…in the negative.

My positive self talk is:

_____
_____
_____

Positive techniques I could use to manage my anger are:

_____
_____
_____

Positive Self Talk Statements

When you change your thinking and self talk, you are more likely to de-escalate your anger and regain your self control.

- I don't need to be "right" in this situation.
- I don't have to prove myself.
- As long as I keep my cool, I am in control of myself.
- I am not threatened. I am in control.
- I cannot control other people or their feelings, but I can control my own.
- I don't need to be in control of everything, only myself.
- If people criticize me, it's okay. I will survive.
- I don't have to respond to someone else's anger.
- When I feel angry, I am usually hurt, feel fear or surprise… a feeling happened to trigger my thoughts which moved me into behavior.

Benefit of The Doubt

When you feel your anger starting to rise, put the brakes on it. Calm yourself by squashing the inner critic and look for alternative explanations that might account for the situation you're upset about. Talk to yourself about why it is important that you stay calm.

I need to give this situation the benefit of the doubt because:

- I don't want to ruin my health by increasing anger
- I don't want to lose my job or alienate my boss.
- I don't want to hurt my family or spouse.
- I don't want to lose my friends or co-workers.
- I don't want to wind up in jail or court.
- I don't want to be a bad example to my children.

Time Out!

As part of your anger treatment plan agree to take a temporary time-out when confronted with an angry situation. Take the opportunity to step away from the situation to give yourself some space and time to calm down. Taking a time out will allow you to evaluate the situation with a more rational perspective.

A time out simply means that you are taking a break from a situation when you feel yourself getting angry, stressed and physically tense. The goal is to get away from the situation so that you can relax, think, cool down and avoid acting out in aggression. How do you take a time out?

- Tell the other person you are feeling tense and need time to calm down and think.
- Remove yourself from the situation or person.
- Keep your time out to a half an hour (or slightly longer if needed). It will take time for your body to return back to normal (heart rate, blood pressure, stress chemicals).
- Do not drive, use alcohol or drugs to calm your self.
- Use the relaxation techniques that you found work best for you.
- Think about what happened to cause your time out. Use rational thoughts to guide you in finding solutions to change the situation.
- Use positive self talk to put your situation into perspective.

If you get back in the game after your time out and you find your anger returning, take another time out. Take as many time outs as it takes to make you feel in control and comfortable with your emotions.

Time Out Questions

Try to answer some of the following problem solving questions while you are on your time out.

- How did I come to that conclusion?
- Are my thoughts true or false?
- How else can I think about the situation?
- Do I see the entire picture or only what I want to see?
- Am I being fair?
- Am I being accepting of others feelings and needs?

Asking yourself questions will allow you to stay in the reality of the situation and not simply use negative self-talk to avoid the real problem.
A time out is a constructive response to anger.

What can I do in my time out to be even more productive?

- Write in your journal. Write about your feelings: what happened to cause the time out? Who caused your feelings: Where did your feelings happen? Why do you feel like you need a time out? What angered you?
- Do something physical such as walking, riding a bike, and running. Physical exercise is the quickest way to decrease your anxiety.
- Sit by yourself and think.
- Wait out your emotions and realize that your feelings come and go.
- Talk to someone you trust.

100

Important Point: A time out means exactly what it says; a time out. It is a time for you to take a break by removing yourself mentally or physically from whatever may be causing your anger. It is a time for you to evaluate and make a plan before acting out in bad behavior. It allows you to have time to step back from the situation so that you can think of a strategy to keep your anger from escalating. Time outs afford you the luxury of thinking about all your options that will keep you in control. As an adult, you have the ability to call your own time outs when you feel your behavior is starting to get out of control.

Physical Time Out Examples

Example: You are home alone babysitting the kids while your husband or wife is grocery shopping. The kids are full of energy, running everywhere and getting on your nerves. You know you cannot leave them unattended, but you need a time out before you lose it.

Plan: Make sure the kids are safe, put them in playpens, put gates up across doorways, assess the room and eliminate any dangers. Step away into the next room (within ear range) and take a time out. Read, relax, walk on your treadmill, think of your positive self talk thoughts.

Example: You are at work and the project you have been working on is getting on your nerves. You can feel yourself starting to feel angry and you are aware of the negative thoughts that keep repeating over and over. You need to get out of there, but you can't get away.

Plan: If it is possible, step away for a short time. Go to the drinking fountain, go to the restroom or go to the break room. Go somewhere for a short time to refocus your mind on something positive. Get away from the situation before you lose control of your emotions and your anger takes over. Stepping away briefly is better than letting your anger build and allowing it to explode.

My physical time outs
are:_____
_____
_____

What If I Can't Take A Time Out

If a physical time out is not possible; try taking a mental time out. You are already familiar with imagery, muscle relaxation and deep breathing from Chapter Three. Try taking four slow, deep breaths. Practice relaxing your muscles and try to keep your body in a relaxed state. Think of your pleasant image. Stop the repetitive negative thoughts that are triggering your angry feelings. Turn the negative repetitive talk into positive affirmations.

My mental time outs are:

_____

_____

_____

Gilligan

Time outs are not designed for you to go on a three hour cruise and never return to the situation. Set a time frame for your mental and physical time outs. Usually a half hour to 45 minutes is a good goal for taking time away to think.

Many anger management students have told me they feel like taking a time out is running away from the issue or problem. *Clarification*: time outs are not designed for you to run away from your problems, ignore problems or hope they disappear and solve themselves. Mental and physical time outs are used to take you away for a short time so you can think of options, deescalate your anger, practice positive self-talk and to make plans to solve your problem. Time outs are for living in solutions and moving beyond the problem.

Your problems and frustrations will be waiting for you when you return from your time out; however, because you have had time away you will be in a better place to handle your emotions. You will have a clearer, more relaxed mind to come up with positive solutions to your problem while at the same time keeping your anger under control.

Getting Back In The Game

When you are ready to come back after a time out, check in with whoever or whatever caused you to take a physical time out. By checking in, you are showing that you are not simply running away from the problem, but taking productive time away from the situation to calm your anger. Make it a priority to not ignore your problems or anger hoping they will go away. Problems will *never* go away without your attention and energy. Without a solution to the situation, your anger will only escalate into stronger levels of emotion and you risk acting out in bad behavior rather than living in solution.

Ask For What You Need

Sometimes the stressors of your work or home can pile up to a point where you feel like you need a time out away from it all. As you learned in the last chapter, if coming home and getting jumped on by all those anxiously awaiting your arrival is a stressor, ask (schedule) for a ½ hour to do something for yourself before you join in the second half of your day. It is always a good idea before taking time away to relax to first let everyone how glad you are to see them and how much you missed them today, but right now you need some time to unwind from your day. Explain how you can't wait to join them, but you first need a little time to shift gears before you jump into any activity.

Find a quiet place to relax, take a bath, read the paper or any activity that you enjoy to help you unwind from the day and make your life a more pleasant place to be. You could take this time to practice your relaxation techniques, engage in an activity you enjoy, exercise, work outside...

Make a plan *not* to rush yourself into stressful situations. For example, if you are trying to make plans for dinner with friends, don't get home at 6 o'clock and agree to meet them at 6:15. Ask for what you need. If you need one hour to unwind, shower and get ready, tell them you will meet them at 7 o'clock.

Don't set yourself up for failure by agreeing to things that you already know causes you to experience stress. Most people are not successful mind readers and if you don't ask for what you want, I'm fairly sure you are not going to get your needs met by others.

An important point! Remember, time outs and running away are two very different things. Again, time outs are for you to make decisions, evaluate your needs and determine how you are going to solve problems. Running away is hoping the problem will go away by itself and never addresses the issue. Running away isn't just about taking yourself out of a situation physically. Running away could also mean altering your mind with drugs or alcohol as an escape. Guess what? When you come back to reality you haven't solved a thing. Don't rely on chemicals to take you away. Rely on your rational brain to help you through the situation.

You May Not Be The Only One

Consider that others in your household may need a time out from their daily stressors as well. Take turns so that everyone can have a break and take time away to refresh themselves from their thoughts and stressors of the day. A dedicated daily ½ hour to de-stress is very necessary for everyone. When you take time for yourself, to check in and live in solution you are ultimately building the healthy inner voice and your self esteem.

The Importance Of Self Esteem

How we feel about ourselves affects virtually every aspect of our experience, from the way we function at work, in love, in friendships, to the way we operate as parents, to how high in life we are likely to rise. Our responses to events are shaped by who and what we think we are. Self esteem is the sum of self confidence and self respect.

Self esteem is how you feel about yourself as a person. Your self esteem may be high or low depending on how much you like or approve of yourself and how much you allow the inner critic into your life. If you have good self esteem, you accept yourself for who you are, both your good qualities and those you consider bad ones. You don't need to impress others because you already know you have value.

People with good self esteem:

- Hold themselves worthy of love.
- Have a healthy inner self.
- Able to state clearly who they are and what they need.
- Look to life with excitement and challenge.
- Set goals for themselves and work toward those goals.
- Accept responsibility for their behavior and consequences.
- Are skilled in dealing with others and forming positive relationships.

People with low self esteem:

- Consider themselves unworthy.
- Are poor problem solvers.
- Are fearful of conflicts with others.
- Experience irrational beliefs and tend to think irrationally.
- Become emotionally stuck.
- Need the approval of others.
- Are unassertive in their needs.

The primary cause of your low self esteem goes back to your childhood. Your parents had the most significant influence on how you feel about yourself today. When parents are loving, encouraging and fair-minded, and provide proper discipline and set appropriate limits, the children they shape end up with good self esteem and are self confident. But when parents are neglectful, critical, unfair, and provide harsh discipline and inappropriate limits, the children they shape are insecure, self critical and suffer from low self esteem.

To raise your self esteem and feel better about yourself you need to figure out who you are, not who you were told to be, the person you are right now. In your journal start writing about who you are, your personality traits, notice when you try to hide the real you. Continue practicing your healthy inner voice and become your own nurturing parent. Set limits for yourself so that you can empower yourself, feel clear headed, and safe. Pay attention to yourself: practice relaxation techniques, implement fun in your life, journal. Increasing self esteem will make a difference in your life. When you are clear on the difference good self esteem will make in your life, you will continue committing yourself to the journey.

Assignment For The Week

Continue writing in your journal.

Make time to practice relaxation techniques.

Come up with a thought stopping saying that you can remember to say when you are beginning to feel anger.

Be aware of negative thoughts and turn them into positive thoughts.

Ask for a physical time out.

Think about the following questions:

What is conscious thought stopping?

What techniques can you use to stop your negative thoughts?

How will you implement a mental or physical time out into your daily schedule?

Are you able to get back into the game after your time out?

Remember to look for your positive progress. Congratulate yourself when you do something well. Recognize your achievements. This is a tough process, but you are here and you are doing it.

What good things happened to you during the week? What did you like about your week/day? What worked for you today? What do you like about your life? What do you like about yourself?

Key Point: If you are feeling overwhelmed by family demands when you return home from work try to make it part of your anger management plan to give yourself some time to decompress before becoming involved in family activities. That could mean working out for a half an hour. That could mean reading a book for 10 minute or listening to music. A few minutes of alone time or a time out will help you to better handle the situations you may face at home.

Key Point: People usually stop thinking clearly when they are angry or upset. Angry people tend to make up their minds about a situation right away, and then spend a great deal of time focusing on how they feel and how the situation affects them that they forget to pay attention to anything else. Instead, work on taking your attention off of your hurt and angry feelings and work on understanding the situation.

Key Point: You do not need to respond to every anger-provoking situation or anger invitation. Take time to gather yourself and collect your thoughts. Your brain is a powerful tool in this process. The more you are able to pull back and approach a troubling situation in a prepared and relaxed manner the more likely you are to get what you want out of that situation.

Chapter 8

Old Techniques And Moods

- Repeating negative self-talk will only allow your anger to become stronger and more unmanageable.
- Replacing negative with positive self-talk will help you keep your emotions under control.
- Taking a time out is a good way for you to relax and gives you time to reassess the situation.
- A physical time out does not mean running away from your problems. Set a time limit for your time out and keep it.
- Make positive self-talk personal to you. Think of a word or phrase to help you stop the negative thoughts/behaviors.
- A mental time out is used to refocus your thoughts when you are unable to remove yourself physically.

Out With The Old And In With The New

Throughout the past few weeks, you have been learning new techniques to aid in keeping your anger under your own control. At this point, you might be asking yourself a few questions about your behavior: How can I change my behavior if I still don't know what behavior to change? What if I'm not sure how I express my anger? How do I cope with bad feelings? How can I change my behavior if I can't recognize how I act out when I am angry or having a bad feeling?

I am confident, since starting this program you learned that everyone has a unique way of dealing/coping with their emotions. Throughout your lifetime you learned how to deal with your bad feelings or cover up your emotions using either your favorite healthy or unhealthy coping styles. Your next challenge in this anger management process is to decide how you display your anger and which anger coping style you rely on to express your anger. As you read through the next section, try to determine which behaviors you use as a method to *cope* rather than *deal* with your anger.

Ways Of Coping With Anger That Do Not Work

As you look through the following coping styles: stuffing anger or passive behavior, indirect or passive-aggressive behavior, acting out or aggressive behavior, it is important to remember that no one fits into only one anger/coping category. Most of you will notice that you use one or more of the following techniques in coping with your anger. The more you are able to recognize and understand each of the different coping styles of anger, the more likely you will be able to move into healthier coping solutions.

The Stuffers (Passive)

Passive behavior is the exact opposite of aggressive behavior. If you have passive behavior, you are allowing things to happen in your life without making any effort to stop or change them. You go along with the crowd even when you don't want to go along with the crowd. On the outside you look happy, but on the inside you are miserable and angry because you allowed yourself to get involved in a situation you would rather not be involved in.

You avoid conflict at all cost. Passive behavior avoids any action that could improve a situation because you put the rights of others ahead of your own. You are too frightened to push for what you really want because it might cause conflict with the needs of others. You would rather shun anger and conflict than to use anger productively in your life.

What's Wrong With That?

Constantly putting the rights of others ahead of your own will diminish your self-worth because your own needs will never be met. You allow resentments to build inside of you because you never let others know what is important to you and it leaves them guessing on how you feel. *You* feel invisible. Stuffers (passive) never set limits and often times feel taken advantage of because they can't say *no*!

Most passive people think they are conquering their anger by not expressing bad feelings in the moment. If you don't express your feelings, they must not exist right? Wrong! When you stuff your anger, you are only setting yourself up to relapse back into unresolved anger later. Unresolved anger escalates and gets stronger with silence. Many stuffers cope with their pent up emotions by using drugs, food or alcohol to numb the feelings rather than dealing with conflict.

What Does Passive Behavior Look Like?

On the outside, you look good and appear sweet and compliant, but on the inside you are feeling helpless and angry because your needs are never met.

Passive behavior is:

- Keeping angry feelings inside instead of doing something to make the situation better.
- Avoiding offending others at all costs by never having conflicts.

- Means you say nothing and therefore never get your own needs met. People rarely argue with you because you appear satisfied.
- You become resentful because no one seems to give you what you want.
- You give anger complete control over you instead of you controlling your anger.

Passive people are and usually:

- Do not like to fight.
- Let their anger build and build.
- Rationalize angry feelings away.
- Try to please everyone.
- Instead of expressing anger openly, you smile, ignore it and seethe on the inside.

Passive Example

Ron hasn't had a Saturday off for two months. Since he is off this Saturday, he made plans with his kids to go to the park, have a cook out and play games.

On Friday night, Ron's sister calls and asks him if he could come over tomorrow around noon to move her washer and dryer. Hauling around heavy equipment is not Ron's favorite thing to do. In fact, he down right hates it. The thing that really makes him angry is his sister never calls for any other reason than to ask him to do work for her. She never just calls to say hello or see how the kids are, it's only about her in every conversation.

On Saturday, at noon, Ron went to his sister's house to move the washer and dryer. Because he felt angry about missing his only Saturday to be with his kids, he communicates with his sister in short, curt; one word answers and complains that his back is killing him.

After Ron moved the washer and dryer, his sister gave him the name of her new doctor to have his back examined. She told him that she had to leave now because she was going out to dinner and that she would see him later.

Is Ron an anger stuffer?

Write about a time when you stuffed your anger and what it made you feel like to allow the anger to grow on the inside:

_____

_____

_____

The Indirect

Passive Aggressive

Passive-aggressive behavior is sort of like being aggressive in a passive way. People who use passive aggressive behavior are not passive one minute and aggressive the next. Instead they use both behaviors cleverly at the same time. Passive aggressive people learn they can frustrate others by simply doing nothing! They conveniently forget, stall, fail, until others give up and quit expecting anything from them.

Passive-aggressive people are good at avoiding conflicts and often express thoughts and feelings that are socially unacceptable. Because you lack self-confidence to ask for what you really need and want, you make yourself appear passive to remain the "good guy" by conveniently forgetting, using jokes at the expense of others and habitual lateness as just a few of the many ways to show your hostility in a sneaky and covert way.

Passive aggressive behavior is difficult and frustrating to identify because you are never really sure where the passive aggressive person is coming from. For example, you confide in your best friend that you desperately need to lose weight. You are so miserable with your recent weight gain that you have decided to buckle down and do something about it because you feel terrible about yourself. She tells you she will work with you in any way she can to help you reach your goal. Throughout the next few weeks, you notice that your friendship has been having its ups and downs. Your friend is bringing you all kinds of delicious desserts and foods. You notice there is a tension in the air, but you aren't sure what the problem is. You sense your friend is angry, but you have no clue why or even if she is angry. When your birthday rolls around your friend happily presents you with a huge box of dark chocolate maple creams. Where is she coming from? Sabotaging your diet? Did she really just forget, conveniently? Did you perhaps anger her and she is passively making a statement? Is she holding on to resentment? Is she really trying to say something to you in giving you candy while she knows you are on a very strict diet for your happiness? Confused?

Passive aggressive behavior is sugar coated hostility.

What's Wrong With That?

Passive aggressive behavior involves you becoming aggressive and expressing your anger indirectly with outbursts that usually have nothing to do with the real issue that is bothering you. Passive aggressive behavior allows you to hide your hostility by agreeing and looking like the nice guy. Passive aggressive behavior helps you to act opposite to what others are expecting. Most people don't want to be around you or form bonds with you because your messages of anger and hostility are confusing. You leave others feeling manipulated. Passive-aggressive behavior lacks honesty.

What does passive-aggressive behavior look like?

Passive aggressive behavior helps you to appear innocent. You can avoid confrontation because you never really tell people you are angry, you just jab them when they least expect it.

How can you look passive and still get back at people (aggressive) without actually telling them that you are angry? You can use sarcasm, teasing, giving them a guilt trip, make others feel like it is their fault or anyway you can think of to hurt and annoy them. In other words, your actions leave others confused and wondering if they are crazy. You use any tactic to avoid the real issue head on.

Passive-Aggressive behavior is:

- Directing your angry feelings at someone or something that had nothing to do with why you are angry.
- Displacing your anger onto loved ones because they are an easy target and usually more accepting of your behavior.
- Finding fault with others.
- Blaming others for your own short comings.
- Using annoying behavior to get back at someone.
- Hiding your current anger and then showing your anger about something totally different.

Passive-Aggressive people are and usually:

- Use manipulation to get back at someone.
- Hide unacceptable behavior so they cannot get blamed for being aggressive.
- Make people feel like their bad behavior was an accident and unintentionally hurtful.
- Hurtful to others by using sarcasm, guilt, excessive teasing
- Use indirect ways to tell people how you feel.
- Seek revenge by agreeing and looking good, but never following through with promises.
- Tell people what they want to hear even if they don't believe in what they are saying.
- Are out of touch with their inner feelings.

Passive-Aggressive Example

James had another very long and hard day at work. He worked 14 hours in a very high stress emergency department and when he got home he was hoping to eat and relax for the rest of his evening. Instead, he found the house in a total mess.

His wife had been talking for over an hour on the phone to her sister who was just there the night before. Toys were everywhere, dogs and cats running wild without food and water and the kids were mud from head to toe. Although James was exhausted, he smiled at his wife and started picking up the house and cleaning up the kids.

After his wife got off the phone James was *hoping* she would make him something to eat. Instead, she turned on the television and started watching her favorite evening show. Instead of asking for her help and thinking she *should* know that he is tired and hungry after working all day, James started to make himself something to eat in between cleaning the kids and feeding the animals. Right in the middle of slapping a sandwich together, the phone rang. It was a telemarketer trying to get James to buy something new on the market. Without hesitation, James let loose on the telemarketer screaming, "Why don't you get a life and leave me the hell alone?"

After slamming the phone down, James said to his wife smiling, "Honey, you should get that type of job! You could sit around all day and talk on the phone and we could make money!"

Was James really that angry with the telemarketer or was his anger caused from something else? Do you think that maybe he wanted to tell his wife that he didn't appreciate her being on the phone and allowing the house to be unattended for the day and instead jabbed her with "you should get that kind of job!"

Write about a time when you used passive-aggressive anger and what you felt like:

_____
_____
_____
_____

The Extreme (Aggression)

Aggression is defined as an act of harm doing inflicted consciously and intentionally upon an unwilling victim. When you first hear the word "aggression" you probably think of physical force, a fist fight, an assault with a weapon, or a loud verbal argument between two people. However, aggression can take many forms, such as spreading vicious gossip, ruining someone's reputation or destroying another person's property.

Aggression is the most extreme form of escalated anger and usually involves standing up for your rights, defending your position or beliefs, while violating the rights and self-worth of others. Aggressive conversation often makes use of "you" statements rather than "I" statements, is blaming, attacking and does not allow the other person to defend their own opinions. When your anger reaches the level of aggression, you are putting yourself in a situation where your actions may easily escalate into a violent action. When you rely on an aggressive approach toward others in a heated situation you run the risk of a knock-down-drag out fight. When you attack others aggressively, either verbally or physically, what you get in return is fear, anger, retaliation, and more aggression all leading to an even more negative outcome. Aggression breeds more aggression.

What's Wrong With That?

The good part about aggressive behavior for you is that you usually get what you need and want through intimidation. The not so good part is you pay a very high price for it. The price you pay is people will fear you and not want to form close bonds with you. People will avoid you at all costs and maybe even plan ways to retaliate against you out of fear.

Energy Release

Research has supported the idea that aggressive anger leads to a high energy state that can last for hours or even longer. Venting your anger (shouting. screaming, punching, kicking, slapping etc) can produce a release of high energy and rid you of pent up emotions. Aggressive physical actions tend to lower the level of anger arousal and the feeling of release can become necessary and addicting to some anger sufferers. Aggressive behavior feels good and sometimes necessary because of the relief experienced after the "letting go," "blowing off steam," "getting rid of," and "letting it all hang out" actions. There are other, more healthy ways, to get the same relief as aggressive behavior with energetic activities.

Energetic activities can use the same amount of energy and help dissipate the extra arousal as acting out in bad behavior. Try exercise, walking, running, sports, physical labor, or other energetic activities especially those that make you feel good. Remember in previous chapters when we talked about living in solution and planning for anger? Implementing physical activity in your daily schedule is an excellent means of releasing pent up stressors and emotions in a healthy setting. If you haven't already, think of some physical activities you can implement into your day to release tension and stress.

Aggressive behavior makes you feel guilty, shameful and remorseful. Sometimes the remorse you feel after violently acting out is more anger provoking than the actual event that angered you in the first place. Feeling guilty, shameful and remorseful over and over because of your unattended behavior drastically lowers your self esteem. When you act out aggressively, you may even feel resentful toward the person you offended because you have put yourself in the bad position of having to apologize to that person. Apologies can be rough when you don't really understand your behavior and its affects on others in your life. Aggression becomes a vicious cycle when left unattended.

What does aggressive behavior look like?

Aggressive behavior is:

- Aggression is a physical response to your anger.
- Aggression is a physical release of pent up energy.
- Not respecting others boundaries.
- Violent.

- The inability to control your impulses (throwing, pushing, slapping).
- Criticizing others.
- Using violent, graphic and vulgar language.
- Feeling powerful by belittling others.
- A strain on relationships with your co-workers, family and friends.
- Extremely unpleasant to be around.
- Acting out aggressively makes you feel guilty and you are always in the position of trying to "make up for it."

Aggressive people are and usually:

- Demanding and pushy.
- Act superior to others.
- Things must go your way without compromise and when they don't go your way, you become loud and intimidating.
- Bossy and controlling to friends, co-workers and family.
- When you verbally attack someone, you escalate into yelling and screaming, use violent language and make threats.
- You are a bully.

Why Use Aggression?

The powerful rush of adrenaline that accompanies anger feels good, storing up bad feelings doesn't. Aggression temporarily and immediately releases the exaggerated pent up energy. Even though this release of energy does not last long, the good feeling may be hard to give up unless you can find another way to relieve your aggressive behavior.

Recap: think of other ways to release the build up of the energy you experience when you have aggression. Take a physical time out! Get rid of the extra energy by power walking, jogging, swimming, riding a bike, hiking, exercise videos, one-person racquetball. Use activities that are non-aggressive and non-competitive.

List of activities I can use to release my energy are:

_____
_____
_____

Write about a time when you used aggressive behavior and what you felt like:

_____
_____
_____

We all resort to some unhealthy ways of dealing with our anger from time to time. The problem becomes when you get stuck in an anger style (passive, passive-aggressive, aggressive) to the point that you prevent the normal use of anger on a daily basis. When you get stuck in an unhealthy anger style, you are unable to adapt to situations. When you get stuck in an unhealthy anger style you become rigid and you are forced to respond the same way over and over again even when it produces negative results.

Changing how you handle your anger can be one of the most important changes you'll make in your life. Clients whose lives and the lives of their families were once nearly ruined by their inability to control their anger found ways to contain and control it and stopped being abusive to their loved ones. Instead of losing control and hurting those around you, stuffing your feelings or giving inaccurate explanations you can learn to identify what triggers your anger and find appropriate ways of handling it.

Moods

What do your moods have to do with your anger? The way you experience your anger or any other emotion can be very much affected by your mood. The biggest problem in experiencing moods is they greatly affect your awareness that you are potentially hurting yourself with your own thinking; especially when you are in a low mood.

On your high mood days, you tend to view your problems dramatically different compared to the days when you are feeling low down and pessimistic. When you are in a high mood, things look good, optimistic and you have a sense of lightheartedness about you. When you experience a problem in a high mood day, you deal with it by finding creative solutions. Life feels good to you and you move on from the problem with a renewed sense of accomplishment. And, you move on in your day with a rational and positive thought process.

When you are in a low mood, everything seems difficult. You become pessimistic, irritable, and defensive and overall your life's problems look insurmountable to you. Your low mood produces low mood thinking and life seems too difficult to even consider a possible solution. Your cycle of negative self talk begins and without your intervention can produce more irrational thoughts and reactions. You can't seem to move on in your day because you are allowing your repetitive negative self talk to take over and chart your destiny.

The fact that you are having a low mood isn't really the problem. Moods come and go. The problem is what you decide to do with your low mood. If you already know that you are in a low mood and negative thinking seems to be taking over, you need to consciously shift into a solution: Do I add to this negativity by joining in with my thinking or do I recognize that I am in a low mood and protect myself from my own thinking? Do I recognize that I have little wisdom when I am in a low mood or do I simply allow the negative thoughts to become my truth? Just as you have a choice in how you display your anger, you also have a choice in how to handle your low mood thinking.

114

When you know that you are in a low mood, you know in advance that things are going to look much different to you than if you were in a high mood. The question to keep asking your self in a low mood is: are these problems *real* problems or are these problems *mood related* problems?

Solution thinking in low moods:

- Try not to overreact to your thoughts when you are feeling low.
- Recognize when you are in a low mood.
- Wait until you feel better to make major decisions.
- Don't trust your wisdom in a low mood.
- Realize that most things, even the good, will look bad in a low mood.
- Try not to take yourself too seriously in a low mood.
- Remember that tomorrow will bring a renewed state of mind.
- Realize that moods come and go.
- Try to avoid serious life changing conversations in a low mood.
- Don't fuel the low mood by your own thinking.
- Don't fight the low mood, recognize it and let it go.

We all want to believe in our thinking and feel justified in our thoughts. The key in trusting your thoughts is to know when your moods are affecting your thinking and realizing that the quality of your thinking is much different in low moods. Pay close attention to your moods. Delay heavy conversations and solving problems when you are in a low mood. Low moods won't last forever. Wait it out. Your high mood is right around the corner and so is your rational thinking.

Feeling Guilty For Being Here

I have heard time and time again that people who are required to take anger management or are asked to take anger management feel a real sense of guilt and shame for what brought them here. Let me assure you that there is not a person in the world that hasn't had problems from time to time managing their anger and I often tell my clients that it isn't really how you got here that matters, rather it matters where you go from here.

Why are you feeling guilty? People usually feel a sense of guilt when they realize that they have done something wrong. Unhealthy guilt cripples those who constantly hold themselves responsible for negative past events. When people live in constant guilt they experience depression, allow themselves to be locked into the past, suffer from low self esteem and punish themselves with poor relationships, excessive eating, drinking, drug use and smoking.

Guilt Is:

- Feeling of regret for your real or imagined misdeeds in the past and present.
- Sense of remorse for thoughts, feelings and attitudes.
- Feeling of loss and shame for not having done something to someone or doing something that negatively impacted your life and lives of others.
- Feeling of responsibility for negative circumstances.
- Feeling obligated to please someone else.

Guilt Can:

- Make you become over responsible striving to make things right.
- Mislead you into irrational beliefs.
- Make you over sensitive.
- Make you become overly fearful.
- Make you feel embarrassed for human circumstances.

Guilty Beliefs:

- I do not deserve happiness.
- I am responsible for other's happiness.
- It is my fault if others are unhappy.
- I should always be responsible and giving toward others.
- I should never feel guilty.
- It is important to save face with others.

As awful as guilt may seem, feeling the emotion of guilt can actually produce positive changes in your life. Positive change may come as a result of you becoming aware and recognizing what happened in your past that may have brought you to this place in your life and then shifting your thoughts over toward living in positive solutions. Relieving yourself of guilt isn't about forgetting the past. It is about forgiving yourself so that you can move on into your future. Unhealthy guilt cripples those who chose to live with it as they continually hold themselves responsible for negative past events.

Letting Go Of Guilt

Step 1:
Acknowledge your responsibility in the situation. The first step to being able to let guilt go is to take responsibility for your part in what happened. Even if your actions were well-intentioned and inadvertently caused a bad situation, it's important to admit that your actions have consequences.

Step 2:
Apologize to any injured parties. You're not going to be able to let go if someone else is still hurting. Offer up a sincere apology, explaining that you understand what you did was

116

wrong and what you wish you had done differently. Even if they don't forgive you, you can now forgive yourself.

Step 3:
Let go of guilt and shame that are connected to your past as long as you've made a genuine effort to change your way of living. Let's face it; all of us have done things that cause us shame when we look back at them. But most people learn from their mistakes and make an effort to become a better person for it. You can undo the past.

Step 4:
Make a plan for how you will do things differently in the future. Without having a new way to approach your life, you'll continue to do things for which you feel guilty. The point of letting your guilt go is to start a fresh, new way of living.

Self Forgiveness

Forgiveness of yourself or someone else, though not easy, can transform your life. Instead of dwelling on the injustice and revenge, instead of being angry and bitter, you can move toward a life of peace, compassion, mercy, joy and kindness.

We have to be willing to forgive ourselves. Holding on to resentment against yourself can be just as toxic as holding on to resentment against someone else. Recognize the fact that poor behavior or mistakes don't make you worthless or bad. It makes you human.

Self Forgiving Is:

- Accepting yourself as a human who makes mistakes and has faults.
- Letting go of self anger for past failures, errors and mistakes.
- No longer punishing yourself for your past and feeling regretful.
- Loving yourself even through your mistakes and misdeeds.
- Lightening the burden of guilt.

Lack Of Self Forgiveness Can Result In:

- Chronic attacks or angry outbursts against yourself.
- Disrespectful treatment of self.
- Self destructive behaviors.
- Indifference toward yourself and your needs.
- Loss of self love.
- Depression.
- Passive aggressive behavior.
- Unwillingness to change.

In Order To Forgive Yourself You Need To Practice:

- Letting go of past hurt and pain.
- Overlooking slight relapses or steps backwards.
- Developing trust in yourself.
- Believing that you are capable of change.
- Building a positive, healthy inner voice.
- Replacing irrational beliefs that block your ability to make positive change.
- Trusting in your goodness.

Forgiveness of yourself or someone else, though not easy, can transform your life. Instead of dwelling on the injustice and revenge, instead of being angry and bitter, you can move toward a life of peace, compassion, mercy, joy and kindness.

Taking Anger On The Road

"He cut me off." "She wouldn't let me pass." "Nobody gives me the finger and gets away with it." "I wouldn't have shot him if he hadn't rear ended me." "He practically ran me off the road, I had no choice."

Have you heard these comments before? Have you even used them yourself from time to time? Have you chased after someone who wronged you on the road to teach them a lesson? Anyone can become an aggressive driver given the right circumstances. Most road warriors don't think they have a problem with anger in their daily lives much less on the road.

Behind The Wheel

Experts say aggressive driving behaviors are triggered by a variety of stimuli. Some are provoked by the actions of another driver; others are set off by roadway congestion. But, most are caused by the drivers' own moods and reactions when they get behind the wheel.

Everyone could probably admit to feeling signs of anger when they get behind the wheel of a car. There is the slow older driver that puts on her signal three miles ahead of time, the tailgater who knows you need to get in a different lane and won't let you get over, the slow driver in the passenger lane that goes 45 miles an hour and you have 10 minutes to make the meeting. Who wouldn't start to feel irritated?

As you learned from the very beginning of this program, irritation is the very first warning sign that you need to mentally take note of your surroundings. Quickly try to determine what is irritating you on the road and try to decide if you have control over it. Take slow, deep breaths, practice a relaxation technique and if all else fails, exit off the freeway into a safe area and take a walk. Give yourself a break when your surrounding becomes too overwhelming.

118

If you decide that other drivers are causing your irritation, get away from them, slow down, change lanes... Since you don't have control over them, you can't teach them a lesson no matter how hard you try. You decide what is best for you and best for your safety on the road. You must decide if the idiot on the road is worth your life.

What if the other driver shows signs of road rage? Let him have his way! Retaliating against someone in a car may only lead to endangering yourself and others. Remember all drivers are equipped with a dangerous weapon; tons of steel in their vehicle. Millions of motorists are also now carrying weapons for protection and tangling with the wrong person might lead to even bigger problems than you can imagine.

Do's and Don'ts

- Do allow people to pass you if they need to, don't block the fast lanes.
- Do leave a safe distance between you and the car in front of you, don't tailgate.
- Do use your signal when you want to change lanes, don't cut drivers off.
- Do keep your hands on the wheel, don't use hand gestures.
- Do use your horn when it's appropriate; don't lay on it for small mistakes a driver may make while on the road.
- Do pay attention when you are on your car phone, don't irritate others by swerving all over the road while you carry your conversation.
- Do let others drive the way they want, don't engage with those who want to race or are antagonizing you.
- Do try to keep your car comfortable (air conditioning, heat, radio, tapes); don't listen to anger inducing talk shows.
- Do know that you can't control the traffic, don't react to it.
- Do not drive if you are already angry, tired or upset.

Assignment For The Week

Continue writing about your anger in your journal.

Decide which technique (passive, passive-aggressive, aggressive) you use to express your anger.

Experiment with activities to release your angry feelings and energy.

Implement a daily exercise plan.

Do not react to road warriors and keep your hands on the wheel.

Think about the following questions:

What is passive, passive-aggressive and aggressive behavior? What do each of the behaviors look like?

What physical activities can I implement to release extra energy?

How do I handle my anger behind the wheel of a car?

Remember to look for your positive progress. Congratulate yourself when you do something well. Recognize your achievements. This is a tough process, but you are here and you are doing it.

What good things happened to you during the week? What did you like about your week/day? What worked for you today? What do you like about your life? What do you like about yourself?

Key Point: You might be asking yourself right now why do people get hooked on using anger? The answer is the anger rush. The anger rush is the strong physical sensation that comes with getting really angry. The rush is the result of the body's natural fight or flight response to danger with the surge of adrenaline and fast heart rate.

Key Point: The adrenaline boost can help you feel strong and it can put some excitement into your day. In fact, the anger rush is one of the hidden attractions to anger. The anger rush can be as hard to give up as a cocaine high. Some compare the anger rush to a strong drink. Becoming dependant on the anger rush to feel is a serious mistake because you will begin to need the anger rush to feel good, to feel excited, or even alive. You then become a slave to your anger because it is stimulating, attractive and exciting.

Key Point: You can learn to acknowledge your own anger and find ways of speaking up for yourself as opposed to pretending you aren't angry while quietly planning ways to get back at those who have hurt you.

Key Point: Instead of controlling others with your anger you can find healthy ways of asking for what you need (assertiveness).

Key Point: You can learn to focus your anger appropriately instead of taking it out on your family, friends, boss, parents or past relationships.

Key Point: When you learn different ways of expressing your emotions you build your self esteem and you will find that your physical well being will improve.

Chapter 9

Communication 101

- Passive behavior avoids any solution that could improve a situation because you want to avoid conflicts at all cost.
- Constantly putting the rights of others ahead of your own can lead to low self-esteem.
- Passive-aggressive behavior is passive in an aggressive way.
- Passive-aggressive behavior is difficult to identify because it is not consistent.
- Aggressive behavior is uncontrolled anger that escalates into a verbal or physical act.
- Aggressive behavior can make you feel resentful because you are always trying to make things up to people.
- Road warriors have uncontrolled anger problems.
- Being able to spot road rage in others will help keep you safe while you are on the road.

I want to take you back to Chapter One when we talked about the stages of change. You have already been utilizing the first stage which is awareness as well as the second stage called preparation for change. In this chapter, you are going to be moving into the action stage of the process by implementing a different communication style into your life.

You may have asked yourself in the past: How can I get others to listen to me? To better understand your needs and boundaries? How can I communicate in a way so that I feel like a winner when I talk with people?

Right In The Middle

The ability to communicate effectively does not come naturally for most people. In order to communicate assertively, you will need to spend a great deal of time developing an understanding of yourself and learning assertive skills. Even those who consider themselves to be assertive communicators have situations or certain relationships in which they find challenging to maintain their assertiveness. If you want to have successful interactions and communication with family, co-workers and casual acquaintances you need to be able to communicate your messages with clarity using assertive communication.

Assertive communication involves expressing your feelings and requests verbally and non-verbally in a way that demonstrates respect both for yourself and others while maintaining your rights. At the same time, asserting yourself appropriately does not guarantee happiness or fair treatment by others. Nor will assertive communication solve all your personal problems or guarantee that others will react assertively in return. Just because you assert *yourself* does not mean you will always get what you are asking for or that others will always be willing to hear you.

Assertiveness Is...

Assertive communication is the middle ground between passive communication and aggressive communication. The assertive person does not give the message that "You matter more than me" or that "I matter more than you." Instead, they give the message that "We are equals, both of our needs matter, let's find a way to get them both met." When you communicate assertively, you possess the ability to express positive and negative feelings honestly and directly based on the belief that you have the right to be listened to and taken seriously. When you communicate assertively, you have the ability to express your opinions, beliefs and rights without feeling guilty, anxious or in a way that infringes on the rights of others. An assertive communicator also understands that other's feelings, opinions and rights are important, but does not place them either above or below his/her own.

Again, communicating assertively does not guarantee that you will always get exactly what you are asking for or that others will always agree with your thoughts and feelings. What assertive communication *does* guarantee is that you have the right to express yourself with dignity and respect and the ability to say "no" without making excuses or apologizing to others for your needs.

Becoming assertive, like any other skill you have acquired in your lifetime, takes understanding, patience and practice. In order for you to feel more comfortable with your new communication style, you need to practice what you are reading and turn the words into actual skills of daily living. The more you practice assertive communication, the easier it will be for you to express your feelings in a way that maintains your self respect and the respect of others.

What's Good About That?

When you communicate assertively; you command respect from others, you appear confident, straight-forward and honest. Through your words and actions, you let others know they are respected and that their point of view is important. When you behave in an assertive manner you are also reinforcing with yourself and others that your rights and needs are important and deserve to be heard. By sending an assertive message, not only are you being clear with others, but reinforcing your own self esteem at the same time. Assertive communication sends the message that you are deserving and worthy of respect.

Assertive Communication:

- Assertive behavior is the belief that everyone has the right to express his or her own legitimate needs.
- Assertive behavior allows you to say what you need, express your feelings, stand up for your rights, and set appropriate limits.
- Assertive behavior accomplishes your goal. It gets you what you need without violating the rights of others.
- The assertive style allows you to work toward a settlement without anger.
- Assertive behavior makes it possible to seek a solution where both parties get what they want.
- Assertiveness allows you to protect yourself without blaming others.
- Assertiveness allows you set limits without turning people off.

Assertive People Are And Usually:

- See themselves equal in power to others.
- Can express anger without violating the rights of others.
- Respected by others.
- Usually get what they want without attacking others.
- Have a balanced way of getting their needs met. Give a little, get a little.
- Maintain good relationships with others.

Assertive	Passive	Aggressive
Less stress	Stress producing	Stress producing
Problem solving	Problem avoiding	Problem making
Gains respect	Manipulates	Takes advantage
Owns rights	Gives up rights	Disregards rights
Makes choices	Lets others choose	Chooses for others
Self-confident	Low self-esteem	Demanding

Why practice assertiveness?

If you are unable to communicate your needs, you risk:

- Becoming resentful because others will never know what you need or want.
- Building frustrations because your needs are never met causing low self-esteem.
- Growing anger to the point of violence or aggression.
- Because you are unable to express yourself and your emotions, you have poor family relationships.

- Low self esteem.
- Passive behavior.
- Silent anger that will grow into strong anger because you can't express yourself.

Assertive Statement

Assertiveness is about standing up for yourself, believing in your opinions and your right to be heard. At the same time, it is also about respecting the opinions and needs of others. To express yourself assertively you need to be clear in your requests. In order to be clear and assertive with others, you need to know exactly what it is that you want. It's very difficult for others to understand what you're asking of them if you don't understand what you need and want yourself.

It's Not All About Talking

Behaving assertively is not all about what you say in a verbal message, but also about *how* you say it in your tone of voice, and body language. Facial expressions, tone of voice, posture and other body language are all used to reinforce what you are saying and feeling. For example, if you are tying to express yourself while avoiding eye contact with the other person you are communicating your needs passively. Can you really expect your audience to pay attention to your message if you don't even believe in it enough to express it with confidence? If you are yelling and clenching your fists you are expressing yourself with aggression. How likely is your audience to stick around for the end result? Assertiveness sends a message of credibility and self worth.

If you believe that you have rights, you are ready to send your messages with credibility and self worth. When you are confident and believe what you have to say is important, people will believe what they see and hear. You have the right...

I have the right to be assertive
I have the right to ask for what I want.
I have the right to express my own opinions and feelings.
I have the right to make my own decisions.
I have the right to make mistakes.
I have the right to say I do not understand.
I have the right to change my mind.
I have the right to be alone.
I have the right to say 'yes' and 'no' for myself.
I have the right to be treated with respect as an intelligent, capable, and equal human being.

Effective Communication:

- Gives equal amounts of talking and listening time.
- Pays attention to what others are telling you.
- Stays on track with your current feeling.
- Remains open and accepting.
- Expresses your thoughts honestly, leaving no hidden meanings.
- Asks for what you want and why.
- Clarifies for you and the other person exactly what you feel.

Setting The Scene

What does assertive body language look like?

- Maintains direct eye contact. If you gaze around the room or look at the floor, your message loses its value. On the other hand, when you look someone in the eye, you are reinforcing the importance of your message. You are taking what you have to say very seriously letting the other person know that you feel strongly about your issue and it is important to you.
- Maintain an open, relaxed, and upright posture. When your head is down, you appear frightened and insecure. If the other person is sitting; sit. If the other person is standing; stand. Keep yourself on the same level as the other person.
- Speak clearly, calmly and loud enough to be heard.
- Do not continually apologize for your feelings. You have a right to express yourself and you have a right to be heard. No apologies necessary.
- Communicate directly and to the point. Keep your conversation on target.
- Do not drudge up old information or things that happened in the past. Stick with the current situation. No one wants to hear about something they did to you from 5 years ago again and again.
- Communicate openly and honestly and avoid underlying meanings. Don't leave them guessing.

Facts, Feelings And Fair Requests

How do you stay on target in assertive communication? As a guideline; assertive messages are characterized by use of the three "F's": facts, feelings, and fair requests.

The facts lay the issues on the table. Facts are an accurate description of what you see, hear or notice. Facts are what you perceive without adding in your own judgments, placing blame, guessing or mind reading the intentions of the other person. Expressing your feelings in an assertive conversation allows the other person to become aware of how his/her behavior affects you without blaming or bullying the other person into defensiveness. Including a fair request means you are asking for something that you need and want from the other person within reason. Asking someone to change their mind about important moral issues is not a fair request. Your request must be achievable by the other person.

Facts

Step 1 of Assertive Communication:

Stating *just the facts* will allow you to open up a discussion without putting the other person on the defensive. There are no insults, no drudging up of the past, no accusations, no exaggerations of the truth; just the facts. You are also taking responsibility for your facts and feelings by using "I" statements.

"I" statements express your own feelings, opinions or thoughts without blaming or judging others. Through "I" statements you are taking responsibility for your thoughts rather than making broad statements which may not be true for everyone. "I" statements take ownership and command respect. "You" statements place blame and make others want to leave the conversation. "You" statements are conversation stoppers. "I" statements are conversation enhancers.

Using this approach (sticking with the facts and "I" statements) will immediately gain cooperation from the other person because they will feel respected and part of a truthful discussion. Below are examples of assertive statements without feelings or fair requests.

Examples of assertive messages without blaming or judging:

- "I" see that the dog has not been fed yet.
- "I" noticed that there are dirty clothes still lying on the bedroom floor.
- "It looks like the overdue library books are still sitting on the desk."

Now let's look at the same examples without the facts. How you would feel if someone communicated their message to you in this manner?

Examples of non-assertive messages:

- "Are you too lazy to get up and feed the dog?"

- "This place is a pig pen because your dirty clothes are all over the bedroom floor."

- "What idiot keeps overdue library books sitting on their desk?"

These non assertive examples are: insulting, belittling, and name calling. These messages will not only escalate your own anger, but put others on the defensive and ready to fight.

How likely is the other person going to give you what you need or want if your messages are rude and insulting? You begin the conversation with one angry person filled with bad feelings and you end up with two very angry people having an unproductive

126

conversation.

Feelings

Step 2 of Assertive Communication:

The second step of an assertive statement acknowledges your honest reaction; your personal feelings. It clearly lets the other person know how their behavior has affected you.

The goal is to state your feelings in a way that avoids making the other person feel accused and offended. Stay away from comments that blame, cause guilt or judge others. Remember: *you* own your feeling. Placing blame using a "you" statement will not set the stage for a willing audience.

Let's look at the same examples with assertive personal feelings.

- "When I came home from work and saw that the dog was not fed I *felt* angry."

- "When you spend most of your day watching T.V. and not helping out around the house, it takes away time that we could be spending together when I get home. I *miss you* when I am away at work."

- "When I saw the overdue library books sitting on your desk for weeks and weeks, I *felt* resentful that you might not care that our money is getting wasted."

Fair Request

Step 3 of Assertive Communication:

The last step of assertive communication is to include a reasonable fair request. This simply means asking for what you want, keeping in mind there are limitations and guidelines about what is considered a fair request.

First, make sure that what you are asking for is reasonable. "I want you to buy the airline company you work for so we can make our own flight schedules for our vacations." Although pretty clear in what you are requesting and understandable, is it a reasonable fair request? "I want to go on a week long vacation to the East coast this summer. I want to leave in the morning and return in the late evening. Can you arrange those times for us?" This is a fair request because it is reasonable and attainable.

Secondly, make one request at a time. You may really want a new house, the dirty clothes picked up, library books returned on time, new landscaping, the dog fed on time, dinner parties and to spend more time together. While you could probably achieve all of those tasks because they are reasonable, bringing them all up at once can be overwhelming and make the other person feel both criticized and attacked. Keep it simple and one request at a time.

Examples of Assertive Statements Including Facts, Feelings and Fair Requests:

- "When I drove the car to work this morning, I noticed that the gas tank was almost empty. (Facts) I felt annoyed and angry. (Feelings) When you use the car on the weekend, I would like you to make sure that you refill the tank, so I won't be inconvenienced stopping for gas at 6:00 AM" (Fair Request)

- "You spend a lot of time working on projects for the office at home and on the weekends." (Facts) "I feel lonely and miss connecting with you." (Feelings) "I would like to make a date with you for a quiet, romantic dinner this weekend." (Fair request)

Practice

Convert this statement from a "you" to an "I" statement.

"You can't get away with criticizing me in front of my friends all of the time. If you do it again, you'll be sorry."

"I" Statement:

"I get angry when you criticize me in front of my friends. I want you to stop it immediately and never do it again. It hurts my feelings."

Convert this statement from a "you" to an "I" statement.

"You always throw the newspaper all over the floor after you read it. One of these days I am going to slip on it and break my back. Is that what you want me to do"?

_____
_____
_____

Answer: "I notice that after you read the newspaper it stays on the floor for a long time. I'm worried that someone is going to slip on it and hurt themselves. Is there somewhere else you could put it that is out of everyone's way?

Convert this statement from a "you" to an "I" statement.

"You never take me out to dinner anymore. You used to always take me out and treat me special. If you don't start taking me out soon, I will ask someone else to go out with me".

_____

_____

_____

Answer: "I notice that we don't go out much anymore. I really felt special when you took me out to dinner and shopping. Is there any free time this week that we could go out and maybe see a movie or go out to dinner?"

It's Not Always Easy

Using assertive communication is *not* easy especially when you are first learning to express yourself with facts, feelings and fair requests. The only way to gain comfort is to practice. Practicing assertive communication will help you become more proficient and feel more comfortable expressing yourself over time.

Most people have never learned to communicate assertively and may even take offense to your facts, feelings and fair requests. Your job in communicating effectively is to express yourself assertively while maintaining respect for the other person at the same time. It is important to keep in mind that you are not responsible for someone else's bad reaction to what you need and want in your own life. You are responsible for a clear message and others are responsible for their reactions. Assertive communication does get easier with practice and you will lead others by your assertiveness example.

Passive? Aggressive? Assertive?

Read each of the scenarios below and try to determine if they are passive, aggressive or assertive. If you decide the statements are passive or aggression, rewrite the statement to make it assertive.

Someone cuts in front of you in a long line at your favorite coffee shop. You start yelling and screaming at them.

_____

_____

A group of co-workers are discussing a topic that you know a lot about. You want to join the conversation, but you don't because you are afraid your opinions may offend others.

_____
_____

You are out to dinner with a group of friends and you control the entire conversation.

_____
_____

When you need something from family and friends you are able to ask them for help.

_____
_____

You punch people out when you are angry.

_____
_____

When someone makes an unfair request, you are able to refuse.

_____
_____

A clerk talks you into buying something that you don't need or want.

_____
_____

You ask your friend politely to pay back the money he owes you.

_____
_____

Handle the following situations using assertive communication:

You are at a restaurant and the food you get isn't what you ordered.

_____
_____

Someone keeps bumping and kicking your seat on an airplane.

_____
_____

You are having a conversation with a friend who continually interrupts you.

_____

_____

A co-worker stands too close when he talks to you. You do not like people that close in your personal space.

_____

_____

You need help in a department store but all of the salespeople are discussing the party they went to last night.

_____

_____

Important Point: Assertive communication means you are asking for what you need and want and at the same time respecting the rights and feelings of others. If you want people to respond to your ideas and requests, you must communicate in a way that others will want to respond with kindness and respect. Good communication is not all about you talking. You must listen and hear others in the process. A willing audience is your strongest asset.

Remember: Learning a new communication style takes time and practice. Learning a new communication style also requires a willingness to accept yourself as you make mistakes in reaching your goal of an assertive communicator. Once you experience that the world doesn't end when you say *No*, that you have a greater chance of getting your needs met, and that dealing with conflict makes life easier, you'll experience greater control over your choices and your life.

Assignment For The Week

Continue writing in your journal.

Practice communicating assertively whenever you have the opportunity.

Make a list of things you need and want in your life.

Begin to notice your body actions when you communicate. Try to make eye contact, sit erect and remain calm.

Start replacing "you" statements with "I" statements.

Practice sticking with facts, feelings and fair requests in all conversations.

Think about the following questions:

What does assertive communication look like?

Can you tell the difference between passive, passive aggressive and aggressive

behaviors?

Do you understand the difference in "you" vs. "I" statements?

What are facts, feelings and fair requests?

Remember to look for your positive progress. Congratulate yourself when you do something well. Recognize your achievements. This is a tough process, but you are here and you are doing it.

What good things happened to you during the week? What did you like about your week/day? What worked for you today? What do you like about your life? What do you like about yourself?

Key Point: Communicating assertively is the most likely way to ensure that everyone involved gets their needs taken care of.

Key Point: Learning how to become assertive rather than aggressive or passive-aggressive is an important step in discovering how to communicate appropriately with others.

Key Point: People who have difficulty being assertive often also have difficulty making requests.

Key Point: Assertive communication is the middle ground between passive communication and aggressive communication. The assertive person does not give the message that "You matter more than me" or that "I matter more than you." Instead, they give the message that "We are equals, both of our needs matter, let's find a way to get them both met."

Key Point: Assertive communication involves expressing your feelings and requests verbally and non-verbally in a way that demonstrates respect both for yourself and others while maintaining your rights.

Chapter 10

Boundaries

- Assertive communication allows you to say what you need, stand up for your rights and set appropriate limits.
- Assertive messages always include: facts, feelings and fairness.
- Assertive people can express anger without violating the right of others.
- Assertive communication will allow you to have a discussion with others without putting the other person on the defense.
- The goal in stating your feelings is you avoid making the other person feel offended and accused.
- "I" statements takes ownership.
- Assertive communication takes practice to build your comfort zone.

In the last chapter you worked through learning a new language called assertive communication. This chapter is going to keep you in the Action Stage of change by teaching you to implement boundaries.

Don't Just Go Along For The Ride

Do you really mean *no*, but you say *yes* just to be nice?

Do you feel resentful when you are asked to go somewhere and you make yourself miserable by going along even when you don't want to?

Do you take insulting, sarcastic comments from a close friend or family members without telling them that it hurts your feelings?

Do others pile endless amounts of work on you because they know you won't say anything?

If you are agreeing with the scenarios above or could add many more of your own, it is time you learn to set boundaries.

Boundaries And Limits

Boundaries are imaginary lines we establish to protect ourselves from the unhealthy, draining and damaging behavior of others. In other words, your boundaries are dividing lines between you and anyone else that may not be violated. By setting a clear boundary you are informing others of your limits. A boundary also informs others when they are acting in ways that are unacceptable to you. Examples, "I don't appreciate you screaming at me." "It hurts my feelings when you call me names." "I would like you to stop touching me right now."

We all have the right to make choices that we believe will bring us comfort and satisfaction in our lives. We have the right to determine our own values, limits and priorities. The capacity to set limits and establish boundaries is essential in feeling good about yourself and maintaining your self esteem. Learning to set appropriate boundaries is a vital part of communicating in an assertive and honest manner.

Many people tell me they have problems setting a boundary because they feel as though boundaries are rigid restrictions imposed on loved ones, co-workers and friends. Setting a boundary is not disrespectful, bad or wrong. In fact, boundaries make you feel safe and actually prevent you from feeling hurt or angry. Setting a boundary is not an attempt to control the other person although some of the people who you set boundaries with will certainly attempt to make you believe you are trying to control them.

Setting a boundary is part of the process of defining yourself and determining what is or is not acceptable to you. It is a vital responsibility to yourself and your life. When you set a healthy boundary, you are sending yourself a very important message: you are worthy of care and you matter in your own life.

It is your responsibility to take care of and protect yourself by letting others know what is and is not acceptable to you by setting limits and boundaries. You must own your rights and responsibilities as co-creator of your life.

A Boundary Is The:

- Limit or line which you will not allow anyone to cross.
- Healthy emotional and physical distance you can maintain between you and another so that you do not become overly dependent.
- Space you need in order to be the real you without feeling pressure from others.
- Line where you end and another begins.
- Clearly defined limits of which are you free to be yourself with no restrictions.

When do I need boundaries?

How do you know when you need to set a boundary? For most of us, the need to set a boundary occurs when any of the following repetitive behaviors happen over and over again: when you feel blamed, shamed, attacked, rejected, abused, angry, overly explaining, defending yourself or someone else, feeling picked on, being provoked or button pushing, being projected on, and manipulated. These are just a few of the reasons boundaries need to set and maintained.

Paying attention to yourself and how you feel about certain situations in your life will help you realize when you need to set boundaries. If you find yourself doing any of the following, it may be time to work on setting clear boundaries:

- Over looking someone else's bad or irritating behavior.
- Making excuses for yourself or others.
- Not standing up for your rights when you are being taken advantage of.
- Wasting your time by practicing what you are going to say to someone rather than setting a boundary.
- Explaining your position over and over again, hoping to get permission from someone to feel a certain way.
- Letting down your boundaries and feeling hurt or taken advantage of time and time again.

Risky Business

Setting a boundary means that you are taking responsibility, being an adult and demanding equality and respect in a relationship. You cannot simultaneously set a boundary with someone and take care of *their* feelings of hurt, anger or disappointment at the same time. Boundaries are about *you* and what you need in *your* life.

There will also be those who won't like your new boundaries and may simply go away and leave your life. Or, *you* might decide that you need to cut certain people out of your life because of their unwillingness to respect your boundaries or change their unacceptable behavior. Think about and plan out your boundaries ahead of time so you will be ready and willing to accept the outcomes.

Example: A good friend of yours constantly manipulates you into doing things and going places at times that are inconvenient for you. You always give in and go with your friend even if it puts you in a bad position. One day, you decide that you are going to set a boundary and only go with your friend at times that are good for both of you. Once you enforce your boundary, your friend doesn't call as much and isn't as friendly as he used to be. In one way you lost a friend, but in another way you made an important adjustment in your life. If others cannot understand your boundaries and respect what you need and want in your life, it might be time to assess their place *in your* life.

How Do I Begin To Set A Boundary?

You have to know what your boundaries are before you can educate anyone else of your limits. Take time to understand what you need and want in your life and begin by calmly and firmly educating the people in your life about your boundaries. In the process of educating others, be careful not to make them feel wrong or bad for their past behavior toward you. Setting boundaries is not about blaming. Setting boundaries is about you standing up for what you need and want in your life.

The following progressive boundary setting process will help you to educate the people who ignore or continue to invade your boundaries. Begin with Step 1 and move on to the rest of the steps if you feel as though your boundary is continually over looked or ignored.

Step 1. Inform others immediately when their behavior is not acceptable to you.
"I will not allow you to talk to me that way."

Step 2. Ask that they stop the unacceptable behavior.
"Please lower voice when you speak to me."

Step 3. Let them know what you need them to do.
"I need you to stop what you are saying immediately."

Step 4. Enforce your boundaries.
"I demand that you stop talking to me right now."

Step 5. Take time away to de escalate the situation.
"Your behavior is unacceptable to me right now. I am willing to discuss this with you, but only after you have had some time to go away and think about it. I need a break away from you right now."

In the previous chapter, you learned that a successful assertive statement contains three parts: facts, feelings and fair requests. Setting a boundary also has three key components:

1. Define the behavior you find unacceptable. If you…

2. Describe the action you will take to protect and take care of yourself if the person violates the boundary. I will…

3. Describe what steps you will take to protect the boundary you have set. If you continue this behavior, I will…

Example: *If you* continue to speak to me in that tone and become physically abusive to me one more time *I will* leave this relationship. *I will* call the police and I will prepare to defend myself in court.

Successful Ways to Maintain Your Boundaries

We talk about setting and maintaining boundaries in anger management because boundaries communicate what you need and at the same time not allowing others to take advantage of or manipulate you. When you set boundaries you are proactive and in control of your life. As you know, anger management is about getting proactive in your life and finding solutions to make you feel good about you and yourself in the world.

136

Boundary Tips

- Don't jump to the wrong conclusions. Don't assume that people are intentionally invading your boundaries. Remember, most people don't even know what their own boundaries are much less yours.
- How you present yourself and your boundaries will let others know you are holding your ground. Stay calm and firm in your boundaries and chances are even if others don't like your boundaries, they too will react in a calm manner.
- You are not responsible for how others feel regarding your boundaries.
- Use "I" statements to give your boundaries, needs and feelings ownership. "I would rather", "I choose", "I do not".
- Be clear (assertive) when setting your boundaries. Don't leave any room for guess work.

Boundary Practice

You are exhausted from work and cannot wait to go home. You have things you need to finish up on at home and then you are going to take a nice long hot bath and relax. Your co-worker Ann asks you to go to the mall and help her pick out a dress for an upcoming wedding. You tell Ann that you have things you really need to do at home and nicely tell her no. Ann continues to nag you all day making you feel badly because she needs you to help her. Finally after not being able to take it anymore you give in and Ann is thrilled.

Re-write this scenario using assertive communication and boundary setting:

_____

_____

_____

You go to a friend's birthday party where they are serving food and alcohol. You are having a great time, but you do not feel like drinking because you are driving and have to work the next day. Your friend Mark comes up to you with a drink and says "come on, loosen up." You tell him that you really don't feel like drinking tonight because you have to work in the morning and you drove to the party. He keeps pushing and pushing the drinks and even gets someone else to help him out, telling you that you are sissy for not pounding a few back. Reluctantly you take the drink.

Rewrite this scenario using assertive communication and boundary setting:

_____

_____

_____

You go to a large department store and find a great sale on things you don't really need. You remind yourself that you are on a budget, but you can still buy a few things. You get up to the counter and the sales person tells you that you need this to go with that and that to go with this. You tell him that you are on a budget and want only what you picked out. The sales person continues to tell you what a good deal these things are and that they will never be on sale again. Finally, you decide to just buy them to get out of there and you will return them on a day when he isn't there.

Rewrite this scenario using assertive communication and boundary setting:

_____
_____
_____
_____

Steps To Establishing Healthy Boundaries

Step 1: To establish healthy boundaries you first need to do a self-assessment to determine if there are any symptoms of ignored or violated boundaries in your life. Ignored or violated boundaries could be: feeling invisible, feeling like others are smothering you, shyness, lack of privacy, over involved with others, under involved with others. In your journal, write about how you feel when your boundaries are not respected or ignored.

Step 2: Once you identify the ignored boundaries, you need to identify what unhealthy thoughts or irrational beliefs you have which led you to having your boundaries violated or ignored.

Step 3: After you identify the unhealthy thoughts or beliefs, write down affirmations which are boundary builders. (see the list of rights as the end of this chapter).

Step 4: Once you have completed the boundary building behaviors, you will then begin to implement them as you proceed in your relationships at home, work and your social network.

Assertive communication and boundaries go hand in hand. In order to get what you want, you have to ask for it. In order to keep what you want you must set and enforce your boundaries.

Let's review our list of rights:

I have the right to be assertive
I have the right to ask for what I want.
I have the right to express my own opinions and feelings.
I have the right to make my own decisions.
I have the right to make mistakes.

138

I have the right to say I do not understand.
I have the right to change my mind.
I have the right to be alone.
I have the right to say 'yes' and 'no' for myself.
I have the right to be treated with respect as an intelligent, capable, and equal human being.

Assignment For The Week

Continue writing in your journal.

Set a boundary.

Practice communicating assertively.

Make a list of the things you need and want in your life.

Write down how you plan to get the things you need and want in your life.

Make a list of boundaries that make you feel safe.

Think about the following questions:

What are boundaries?

Are your boundaries risky?

How do you set boundaries?

How can you maintain your boundaries?

Remember to look for your positive progress. Congratulate yourself when you do something well. Recognize your achievements. This is a tough process, but you are here and you are doing it.

What good things happened to you during the week? What did you like about your week/day? What worked for you today? What do you like about your life? What do you like about yourself?

Key Point: Boundaries are imaginary lines we establish to protect ourselves from the unhealthy, draining and damaging behavior of others.

Key Point: You have to know what your boundaries are before you can educate anyone else of your limits.

Chapter 11

Putting It All Together

- A boundary is a dividing line between you and anyone else.
- The purpose of having boundaries is to protect and care for your self.
- Paying attention to your feelings will let you know when you need to set boundaries.
- Most people do not know how to set boundaries for themselves much less honor yours.
- When you set a boundary, you are taking a risk that others may not like it.
- State your boundaries clearly and assertively leaving no room for guess work.
- Maintaining your boundaries helps you manage anger.

While you are working to overcome your anger problem, you are likely to experience times when you relapse back into earlier anger habits and find yourself becoming inappropriately angry, confused and feeling defeated. If you do experience a relapse in your behavior, the most important thing you can do is refuse to give up your gains. Don't let a relapse be an excuse for throwing in the towel and quitting. Try to understand your relapse by examining what part of your anger plan didn't work for you. Use that information to fix your anger plan so it will work better the next time around.

Throughout the book we have talked about a number of techniques for managing your anger. When you are faced with a situation that provokes your anger, learn to stop and reflect before responding.

1. Immediately stop how you are thinking and acting at the very moment you start to feel uncomfortable or feel yourself becoming angry.
2. Practice a relaxation technique (deep breathing, imagery, muscle relaxation).
3. Time yourself out.
4. Reflect and try to identify the anger trigger that set you off. Ask yourself:
   What thoughts are going through my head?
   What is my body doing?
   Am I responding to a real problem or to a first impression?
   What would the likely circumstance be if I act out aggressively?
   What are the alternate ways (that I just learned) I could respond to this situation that could resolve the issue?
5. Choose how you want to respond. Work toward assertiveness rather than aggressiveness.
6. Respond with a clear, calm brain.

The End?

I hope this process of anger management will serve as a stepping stone to get you excited and thinking about other ways to improve your life. This whole process has been about you becoming proactive and finding the right solutions for your life. Keep in mind that just because you have reached the end of this book does not mean your mission of anger management is over.

As I mentioned in the very beginning of this book, anger management takes a bad rap from the majority. One of the many reasons anger management takes a bad rap is most of you will start out with a renewed sense of hope. As the days and weeks go by you may start to slip back into old behaviors because you stop paying close attention to yourself. The biggest reason most people stop paying attention to themselves is because this is hard work! Anger management is *very* hard work!

Another reason I notice people stop paying attention to their own life is time passage. As time passes, the reasons you took anger management or the things that lead you to anger management don't appear quite as important as when you first began your process. Slipping back into comfortable behaviors is easy; moving forward in solution is hard work.

Throughout this book and program, you have experienced some exciting changes in your life through own your hard work and effort. There are more exciting changes in your future if you maintain your desire for change. In order to maintain the valuable solutions you have implemented into your life you must think about your self improvements every day and continually look for new ways to enhance your life. Anger management is a life long quest. Keep searching…

You must commit to follow through with your anger management plan and be open to learning and practicing your techniques or implementing new ones. The only way to be successful in managing your anger is to do what it takes to work the steps of your anger plan which leads us to the last stage of change.

The last stage of change is maintaining your gains. The **maintenance stage** of change never ends. During this last stage you come to realize that you are not perfect and that you will make mistakes and act inappropriately, but you can recover from relapses because you have the tools to make the necessary changes in your anger plan. Each time you have a relapse in your anger plan you will learn and grow in your quest of anger management. You can use the tools and strategies you have learned along the way to pick yourself up and make a speedy recovery.

Let's briefly recap each chapter:

Program Overview

Chapter 1

Anger Is A Fact of Life

You can not eliminate anger from your list of emotions! Our goal is not to wipe out your anger, but to learn to manage it so that anger will work for you in a positive way.

The best part about anger is that you are in charge of it and yourself.

With hard work and practice you can learn to change old behaviors that are not working for you anymore and replace them with new healthy solutions.

Learning about your anger requires you to become aware of your behaviors on a daily basis.

Old behaviors, even though they don't work, are comfortable because they have been around for a very long time.

You have the power and control to make your life a more pleasant place to be by learning to manage your anger.

Most of your old behaviors were learned when you were a child by observing the adults in your life and how they expressed their anger.

What you do with your anger and how you choose to display it is entirely up to you.

Anger can create powerful, positive change.

The goal of anger management is to reduce both your emotional feelings and the physiological arousal that anger causes; not eliminate anger.

Chapter 2

Reading The Signs

Understanding when, where and how intensely you feel anger will help you avoid situations that cause you to have strong anger.

The first thing you need to know about your anger is what triggers it, what brings it on and fuels it.

142

The second thing you need to know is how intensely you feel your anger.

Rating your anger (mild, moderate, severe) will help you learn how strong it can get during an angry episode.

Making yourself aware of the intensity of your anger will help you avoid situations that put you at the greatest risk of uncontrolled anger.

The intensity of your anger is a gauge of how you might act out physically when you feel angry.

Make a plan to avoid the things that cause your anger to escalate out of control.

The first step in learning to recognize levels of anger is to become aware of anger cues or anger signs. The better you are at reading the signs the better you will become at rating and managing your anger.

Chapter 3

Warning, Warning!

Warning signs are your first clues to stress and anger. First there is a thought, next is a feeling and then comes a reaction.

Anger warning signs/repetitive negative thoughts are signals that you need to pay attention and check things out before they escalate into more than just a warning.

Not only are you affected emotionally every time you experience anger, your body under goes dramatic chemical changes to prepare you to either run or fight.

Once the chemical reaction occurs you are in your attack mode and ready to fight.

Although we experience strong chemical reactions when we are angry, most situations we are faced with do not require the strong response of "fight or flight."

Chronic anger is constant anger.

The chemicals that are released in your body during the "fight or flight" response can accumulate in your body and make you pay a physical price for being in a constant high energy state.

Recognizing your own behavior is one of the most important processes in learning to manage your anger. Think if angry is the way you want to present yourself to the world or the way you want to feel on a daily basis. Think about the powerful physical changes your body goes through each and every time you experience anger. Think!

Chapter 4

Is It Really Anger?

Experiencing and expressing emotions are an important part of your life.

Properly identifying the exact emotion can be difficult for most people and even more difficult to express appropriately.

Your thoughts, perception and senses all quickly guide you to respond in certain ways when you are experiencing an emotion or feeling.

Your emotional or physical response can be more related to the interpretation of events more than to the actual event itself.

If you can't identify what you are feeling, you risk acting out inappropriately.

Fear, anger and surprise can create the same responses.

Fear: an unpleasant often strong emotion caused by anticipation or awareness of danger.

Surprise: to attack unexpectedly, to cause astonishment.

Anger can be caused by other feelings and emotions.

"Feelings" Word List

Angry	Calm	Hopeless
Frustrated	Happy	Depressed
Hateful	Joyful	Inferior
Irritated	Secure	Rejected
Uncomfortable	Peaceful	Helpless
Superior	Excited	Regret

Recognition is the key in managing your anger. Everyone experiences some type of warning sign when they first start to get angry. Learning to pay attention to the early signs will help you recognize and get your anger under control before it gets out of hand.

144

You control yourself and you control your anger. Quickly control your anger by recognizing that you feel angry, monitor the situation you are involved in and stop your anger from getting out of control.

Chapter 5

Relax

You need to intervene immediately to stop yourself from having uncontrolled behavior.

Deep breathing is the easiest and most convenient way to relax your body.

Muscle relaxation requires you to focus on relaxing your muscles from your head to your toes in a quiet environment.

If you need to take a short time out to relax from your day; take it!

Relaxing imagery is a pleasant thought that you can quickly recall to calm your angry feelings.

Relaxation techniques will help you plan ways to control your anger and keep it manageable.

Chapter 6

More Ways To Calm Yourself

When you repeat negative thoughts over and over you are experiencing negative self-talk.

Negative self-talk can lead to unpleasant emotions and stressful physical responses.

Filtering is focusing only on the negative points of a situation.

Black and white self-talk is all or nothing thinking.

Over generalizing is taking the outcome of one situation and applying it to all other situations.

Mind reading involves making assumptions about what others are thinking without actually knowing for sure.

When you first notice that you are engaging in negative self-talk catch yourself in the act and stop it. Put a halt to negative messages as soon as you first notice them and refocus your thoughts on positive coping thoughts. Justified anger can become quickly irrational anger when you repeat the same negative thoughts over and over.

Chapter 7

Turning It All Around

Positive self-talk is the opposite of negative.

Conscious thought stopping involves putting an end to negative messages as soon as you realize you are experiencing them.

Whenever you have an uncomfortable feeling or emotion; tell yourself to **stop**.

Try to figure out where your negative thoughts are coming from and refocus your mind back to positive self-talk thoughts and feelings.

Try to catch yourself saying or thinking negative thoughts, words or ideas.

Be careful not to exaggerate the situation or your feelings.

Replace irrational thoughts with rational ones.

Make your thought stopping personal to you. Think of an image or a word you can use to stop the negative thoughts and talk.

A physical time out is: time that you take away from a situation to calm yourself and to think of ways to solve your problem.

Set a time limit for your time out.

Negative self-talk can easily go on automatic pilot without you even noticing it. At the very first sign of or becoming aware that your thoughts are repetitive and negative, allow your thought stopping mechanism to kick in. Repeating negative thoughts over and over will only allow your anger to build and your thoughts to become more irrational. Pay attention to what you are saying to yourself!

Chapter 8

Old Techniques

If you have passive behavior, you allow things to happen without making any effort to stop or change them. You avoid conflict at all cost.

If you have passive-aggressive behavior, you avoid conflicts and express your feelings

146

and thoughts in a socially unacceptable way. You appear innocent and avoid confrontation, but you jab at people when they least expect it.

If you have aggressive behavior you use excessive verbal or physical acts against others. You stand up for yourself and your rights in a violent manner.

The powerful surges of energy you get from anger outbursts feels good. Storing bad feelings doesn't.

There are other ways to release the energy from anger such as walking, jogging, swimming, riding a bike. Use activities that are non-competitive and non-aggressive.

If you are already angry, don't get behind the wheel of a car.

Don't cover your emotions with drugs, alcohol or food.

Let others have their way on the road. You can't teach them a lesson. They will learn when they are ready.

Everyone uses a behavior or a combination of behaviors they learn early on in their lives. Learning to recognize and change those behaviors will lead to healthier new way of expressing your feelings and emotions. Don't blame, learn.

Chapter 9

Communication 101

Assertiveness is the ability to openly and honestly express your opinions, feelings and beliefs without infringing on the rights of others.

Assertive communication takes practice and will feel awkward in the beginning.

Assertive communication commands respect from others because you are communicating in an open and honest manner.

Assertive communication uses "I" statements. "I" statements take ownership of your feelings and thoughts.

Listening and paying attention to what others have to say is part of two-way communication.

Assertive messages contain facts, feelings and fair requests.

Being assertive is simply asking for what you need and want while respecting the rights and feelings of others. If you want others to respond to your feelings in a positive way you need learn to communicate them in a positive way. If you want others to show you kindness and respect you must show them kindness and respect. Good communication involves listening to others, expressing yourself assertively and taking responsibility for the things you say.

Chapter 10

Boundaries

A boundary is a dividing line between you and anyone else.

Boundaries clearly let others know what you want, don't want and what you are willing or unwilling to do.

Boundaries let others know when they are acting in a way that is unacceptable to you.

Paying attention to your feelings will help you realize when you need to set a boundary.

You must be willing to take a risk that others may not like your boundary.

Healthy boundaries are flexible.

You are not responsible for how others feel about your boundary.

Assertive communication and boundaries go hand in hand. In order to get what you want, you need to be able to ask for it. In order to keep what you want you must set boundaries and enforce your boundaries.

Pep Talk

It takes real courage and strength to admit that you have an unhealthy anger style and to begin changing it. By working through this book and implementing your anger plan you are taking the first steps to improve your life and I commend you for taking the challenge.

If there were a single thought I would like to leave you with it would be that you *are* capable of managing your anger. When you become proactive in your life, you win the game of anger management. You win the game of anger management when you actively search for solutions that feel good in your life. One of the biggest achievements you can make in your lifetime is living in your own life.

Another important thought I would like to leave you with is while you are working to overcome your anger problem, you are likely to experience times when you relapse back into earlier anger habits and find yourself becoming inappropriately angry, aggressive or belligerent. If you do experience a relapse in your behavior, the most important thing you can do is refuse to give up your gains. Don't let a relapse turn into an excuse for quitting your anger plan or giving up all you have learned. Relapses are learning experiences. Never, ever stop learning new and better ways to improve your life.

It takes real courage and strength to admit that you have an unhealthy anger style and to begin changing it. Along with your courage it takes to make change in your life it is just as important to learn how to put your anger behind you. As we discussed in chapter one, it doesn't matter what brought you here. It matters where you go from here.

Remember: The ultimate goal in anger management is not to eliminate your anger. The goal of anger management is learning to express your feelings in a healthy way which in turn gives you the outcome you desire.

Remember: Anger, as an emotion, is not the problem. It is your behavior as a result of your anger that can get you into trouble.

Remember: Anger management is all about taking responsibility for your anger, learning about it and then finding solutions that are right for your life.

Remember: To change your life, you'll need to commit yourself to changing what you do, pure and simple. Acceptance, compassion, and kindness are never more important than when you deal with barriers. In the past, you may have shied away from difficult feelings, unwanted thoughts, uncontrolled impulses, situations, people, and personal enemies that triggered your anger. You can choose to continue to do that, and you know where that will lead. Or, you can choose to take a different path, one that you can travel on with your head held high knowing that you are living in solution.

It takes two things to change. You need determination and secondly you need the skills to make change. If you made it to the end of this book you have determination and you have the skills to manage your anger. Remember back to the beginning of the book it took everything you had to remember to breathe, relax, practice, try new things? The more you practice the more these skills will become second nature. Stay with your anger management quest and don't neglect your skills. If you feel yourself starting to slip, get right back into your anger plan. The quality of your life and the lives of those you love are so much better now that you have done this work.

Learning to express your feelings and emotions is not a simple process; it is a *life long process*. Recognizing that you need help is the single most important step in learning to manage your anger.

What if I need more help?

If you need more help reach out and get it. Learning to control your anger is not an easy process and many people cannot resolve it alone. Reading this material or participating in an anger management class is a start, but you may also feel the need for help from a professional, someone who specializes in anger management.

Where can you go for help?

Look in your local yellow pages for therapists or counselors listed in your area. Talk to the therapist over the phone and decide if they are someone you might want to work with in anger issues. Interview them.

Ask your family physician if he/she might have a referral.

Call your local hospital and ask if they know of any programs in your area for anger management or if they have therapist referrals that specialize in anger management.

Contact area universities or colleges. Psychology departments sometimes offer counseling services to the community at reduced rates called a sliding scale.

Contact the pastor of your church for his/her recommendation.

Other resources:

National Mental Health Association 800-969-6642

http://www.nmha.org

1-800-Therapist

http://www.1-800-therapist.com

American Association for Marriage and Family Therapists

http://www.aamft.org

Http://www.mytherapynet.com

About the Author

Kathy Garber, R.N./ B.S.N./ M.A., Licensed Marriage and Family Therapist has more than 20 years in the healthcare and mental health industry. She is a Clinical Member of the American Association of Marriage and Family Therapists, a Clinical Member of the California Association of Marriage and Family Therapists. Kathy is a member of The American Academy of Experts in Traumatic Stress and a Board Certified Expert in Traumatic Stress, an honorary member of the Sigma Theta Tau Honorary Nursing Society, a Diplomat of the American Association of Anger Management Providers, a Diplomat of the National Anger Management Association, and Association for Conflict Resolution. She has a background and expertise in "The Lawlis Series" on the Dr. Phil's Approaches.

Kathy works as a Licensed Marriage and Family Therapist, Life and Family Strategist, Certified Anger Management Facilitator, Mediator, Certified Parenting Instructor and Anger Management Evaluator. She works with numerous Probation Departments, Human Resource Departments and psychotherapists across the United States. Kathy enjoys working with individuals and groups teaching successful anger management skills in a variety of settings. She developed and designed http://www.angermanagementonline.com, http://www.angerevaluation.com, http://www.stopangerbehappy.com , http://Family-Intervention.net and is an active director of the programs. Kathy is the Founder and Director of Center of Solutions, LLC. She is the author of Stop Anger, Be Happy and Parenting By Design. Kathy also serves as co-director of http://parentingclass.net an online program designed for divorcing parents working toward resolution in co-parenting. Kathy also works as a family coach and strategist helping individuals with family conflict, reconciliation, family of origin issues at http://www.family-intervention.net.

Made in the USA
Lexington, KY
09 October 2011